D1007679

Assimilating
New Members

Creative Leadership Series

Assimilating New Members

Lyle E. Schaller

Creative Leadership Series
Lyle E. Schaller, Editor

Abingdon Press ● Nashville

ASSIMILATING NEW MEMBERS

Copyright © 1978 by Lyle E. Schaller

20th Printing 1992

This book is printed on recycled, acid-free paper.

Library of Congress Cataloging in Publication Data

Schaller, Lyle E.
  Assimilating new members.
  (Creative leadership series)
  1. Church growth.   2. Church membership.
  3. Commitment to the church. I. Title. II. Series.
BV652.25.S33   254'.5   77-18037

ISBN 0-687-01938-9

MANUFACTURED IN THE UNITED STATES OF AMERICA

To

John and Grace

Foreword

Requests for assistance in encouraging creativity and innovation within congregational life are a part of everyday life for lay leaders, ministers, denominational staff members, and seminary teachers. Church members are aware of the impact of change on the life of the churches, and they seek help in developing a creative response to these pressures.

These pressures take many forms. The pastor feels it in the constant struggle to manage the hours in a day to cover an increasing load of responsibilities. Every few years or so the members feel this pressure as they respond to the departure of their pastor and the arrival of a new minister. The spouse and children of that new minister wonder how they will be received in this new situation. The lay leaders feel these pressures as they grapple with the many facets of stewardship in the allocation of resources. The recent new adult members feel these pressures as they seek to adapt to the life and program of what to them is a new congregation. The leaders are aware of this from the opposite side of that pattern as they seek to help new members gain a sense of belonging. The lay volunteer often wonders if anyone cares about his or her contributions of time and energy. The leaders feel the pressures of replacing the lay volunteers who move away or drop out of a volunteer role and wonder how this can be altered.

These are some of the issues, pressures, questions, and concerns to which this series of books is addressed. The Creative Leadership Series has been prepared to help lay leaders, pastors, denominational leaders, and seminary teachers respond to this growing demand for new insights and greater creativity.

This series is not intended as a problem-solving tool. Rarely do we solve problems. We usually trade one set of problems for a different set of problems. The purpose of this series is to help congregational leaders "trade up" as they exchange one set for a different set.

One of the means of doing this is to understand the context or overall background of a particular issue. Thus Bob Kemper offers to both ministers and the laity an overview of the dynamics involved when a minister begins a new pastorate. This overview can help the new minister avoid some unnecessary pitfalls. It also can help the laity understand the minister's perspective, and that of the minister's family, as they negotiate with, call on, welcome in, and become accustomed to the new pastor.

In this volume I have attempted to provide an overview of both the process and the problems encountered in assimilating new members into a congregation. By looking at this broad picture the leaders can avoid some of the forces which often cause new members to drop into inactivity.

Speed Leas offers the minister a useful frame of reference in looking at the management of time. This frame of reference also can be helpful to the laity in understanding the pressures on their pastor and the constraints of time and energy within which the minister operates.

Doug Johnson describes the general context and climate for volunteers and offers a series of creative suggestions for improving the conditions which encourage and motivate lay volunteers.

Dick Cunningham shifts the focus on stewardship from money to a broader theological definition of that subject and offers a series of challenging and creative insights into a broader and deeper Biblical understanding of the concept of Christian stewardship.

A second means of encouraging a creative response to the issues and questions facing congregational leaders can be found in the admonition, "If you can put a name on it, you can deal with it." The 80-20 rule described by Speed Leas in the volume on time management is an example of this. Another is the cutback syndrome in the third chapter of his book or in the fellowship circle described in the fourth chapter of this volume.

Lyle E. Schaller

Contents

Preface

How can we reach more people with the good news that Jesus Christ is Lord and Savior?—How can we bring them into our church?—How can we help them feel more at home here?—How can we keep our new members from dropping into inactivity?

These are representative of the questions being raised in an age when there is a renewed emphasis in the churches on evangelism, new member recruitment, and church growth. To some extent this renewed interest in the evangelistic outreach of the churches reflects a concern over the decline in total membership of several of the mainline denominational families. It also reflects some frustrations among church leaders over their efforts to reach the young adults of today, who constituted the baby boom of the post World War II era, as well as a basic evangelistic concern.

In looking at the responses to these concerns and to related questions it may be as important to understand the underlying assumptions on which those responses are based as it is to understand the content of what is said or written.

This book focuses on the outreach of existing congregations to people who are not actively involved in the life of any worshiping congregation. It is directed to the leaders, both clergy and lay, of those congregations which are concerned about reaching and assimilating new members into the life and fellowship of that worshiping congregation. This is not a book on new church development. It is not a book on evangelism. It is a book that should help the reader to examine and evaluate the processes for the recruitment and assimilation of new members into the congregation to which that reader belongs. It is a book that should help the reader understand more clearly why some congregations have more difficulty than others in reaching and assimilating new members. It is a book that should help the reader see more clearly what is happening in his or her own congregation in reaching and assimilating new members. This book should help the reader identify and avoid counter-productive behavior patterns. Most important of all, it is hoped that this book will challenge the reader to identify and reflect on his or her assumptions about the evangelistic outreach of the churches, to identify some of the barriers to church growth, and to respond creatively and constructively to many of the most common problems in the assimilation of new members in the typical congregation.

For this to be a productive endeavor it may be necessary for you as reader to articulate and reflect on the assumptions which you carry with you on this subject of reaching and assimilating new members.

It is unfair, however, to ask the reader to do this unless the author of a volume such as this is willing to identify the assumptions on which the book is based. To do so may help the reader understand the perspective and bias of the author, to identify the basic reason behind any difference of opinion between the reader and the author in the subsequent pages, and—perhaps—even help the reader to articulate his or her own assumptions on this subject.

While they are not listed in order of importance, these assumptions are essential to an understanding of the contents of this volume and the reasons behind the sequence in which the material is presented.

First, it is assumed that most Christian congregations in the United States and Canada have the potential for a net growth of at least 5 percent per year. That rate of growth would mean doubling in size in fourteen years since the rate of growth would be compounded annually. In almost every community on the North American continent there are enough people who are not actively involved in the life of any

14

worshiping congregation to make that rate of growth possible.

For example, while in the United States the proportion of adults (age eighteen and over) who identify themselves as Protestants dropped from 71 percent in 1960 to 62 percent in 1976, according to the Gallup Poll, the actual number of self-identified Protestants climbed from an estimated 74 million in 1950 to 82 million in 1960 to 93 million in 1976. During a typical week about 37 million of these 93 million adults attended church at least once. This suggests that every congregation could double its average attendance at worship without even touching the ten million adults who claim no ties to any religious group. In fact, if every Protestant church doubled its average attendance at worship, it would still leave more than twenty million self-identified Protestants as non-attenders for that week. That more than covers those who are in hospitals, nursing homes, sick, traveling, or out of town for the weekend.

Another useful comparison can be found in the fact that approximately 93 million American adults identify themselves as Protestants, but the reported membership of all Protestant churches of all denominations in the United States totals less than 80 million—and this figure includes at least 10 million members who are under eighteen years of age. In other words, the American population includes 23 to 30 million adults who identify themselves as Protestants, but who are not reported as members by any Protestant church.

These are simply two pieces in a huge pile of evidence that suggest Protestant churches have difficulty in reaching and assimilating adults who identify themselves as Protestants. This book represents an attempt to identify some of the factors that keep the Protestant churches from reaching more people with the good news and to suggest more effective approaches.

The second assumption on which this volume rests is that it is good for persons who identify themselves as Christians to be a part of a worshiping congregation. God calls his

15

children to worship him. It is good for the individual Christian to be a member of the worshiping, nurturing, caring, sharing community we refer to as a Christian congregation. Christians are called to live in community—not as hermits. Being a part of that community is a means of nourishing the personal and spiritual growth of the individual Christian. That called-out community gives the individual the opportunity to express that Christian commitment in and through the worshiping congregation.

3) A third basic assumption is that it is not Christian to invite a person to unite with a specific congregation and then not accept that person into the fellowship of that congregation. This process of entrance, acceptance, and assimilation is the major theme of this volume. There is considerable evidence which suggests that at least one-third, and perhaps as many as one-half, of all Protestant church members do not feel a sense of belonging to the congregation of which they are members. They have been received into membership, but have never felt they have been accepted into the fellowship circle.

4) A fourth basic assumption that is a part of the foundation for this book is that evangelism is not necessarily the same as reaching out and receiving new members. It is proclaiming the good news. Every Christian and every Christian congregation is expected to do that by word, deed, and life-style.[1] It is bringing individuals to a personal confrontation with Jesus Christ.

Evangelism is not the same as inviting people to unite with a specific congregation and welcoming them into the nurturing fellowship of that worshiping congregation. The evidence suggests that there are many more adult believers than there are active church members. Evangelism and receiving new members into a congregation are two separate actions. Some congregations are very articulate in proclaim-

---

[1]For a remarkably lucid introduction to the concept of life-style evangelism see C. B. Hogue, *Love Leaves No Choice* (Waco: Word Books, 1976).

ing and witnessing to the good news, but rarely receive new members except for persons who are born into or marry into families in that congregation. Many congregations direct their evangelistic proclamation to one segment of the population spectrum, but receive nearly all their new members from a different segment of the population spectrum. Frequently the evangelistic efforts of a congregation are almost completely unrelated to the processes by which that congregation receives and assimilates, or fails to assimilate, new members.

The fifth basic assumption on which this volume rests is that there is a difference between what God expects of his Church and what God expects of each individual congregation. The church is expected to reach and serve every one of his children. The individual churches each have a distinctive part of that total responsibility, but no one congregation is expected to reach and minister to all the people in the world. One of the popular heresies of the day is that "our congregation" is God's only resource here on this planet.

The sixth, and perhaps one of the three most significant assumptions in explaining the theme of this book, is that nearly every congregation has two barriers around it. The larger outer barrier is composed of several methods, techniques, and traditions that have the combined effect of keeping potential new members from joining that congregation. The first three chapters are devoted to a description of these barriers. One group of barriers can be identified most easily as the organizing of individuals into a cohesive and unified community. Several of these organizing principles usually are perceived by outsiders as exclusionary forces. These are described in the first chapter.

Another group of barriers consists of the unintentional exclusionary dimensions of the congregation. Every congregation, by the nature of the people who are members, by its history and traditions, by the design of the meeting place, by its schedule and program, by its congregational life-style, and by the priorities in the allocation of resources, causes

17

many people to feel excluded. This fact of life constitutes the theme of the second chapter and is touched on again in the last two chapters.

A third group of barriers can be seen in the skills, procedures, techniques, and practices that a congregation develops as a part of its operational system. While these tend not to be perceived as exclusionary or as contradictory to church growth by the members, in fact, many of them do tend to prevent the church from receiving and assimilating new members. A dozen of these are described in the third chapter, and several other counter-productive techniques are identified in the fifth chapter.

A seventh assumption that may help explain what is included in this volume and what is excluded represents a strongly held personal point of view. This is the belief that most people have a greater capability to overcome obstacles, to solve problems, and to change the conditions they are confronted with than they give themselves credit for possessing. Frequently, however, people need help in diagnosing problems and in distinguishing between symptoms and problems. In other words, the central emphasis is on diagnosis—not on prescription—although many prescriptive suggestions are scattered throughout the book, especially in the fourth and sixth chapters.

The eighth assumption overlaps this last one. It is assumed here that in many situations it is more helpful and more productive to ask questions than to offer prescriptions or to give directions. Therefore there is a series of questions at the end of each chapter. These questions are intended to be used by the reader in diagnosing what is happening in a specific congregation. Obviously they are loaded questions, for each question carries with it a value or a bias. In many congregations these questions can be used by an evangelism task force or the membership department or a self-study committee.

The ninth assumption on this list is there is a natural tendency in every organization to place survival goals and institutional maintenance at the top of the agenda. Frequently this pattern not only is tolerated, it also is encouraged by the leaders of that organization or institution. The worshiping congregation is not immune to this expression of cultural religion and institutional blight. A common result is a congregation begins to seek new members in order to perpetuate that institution, rather than to be responsive to the needs of the people that congregation is seeking to reach. The typical result is an effort to "sell our church" to that prospective new member rather than to be sensitive and responsive to the needs of that individual. One result of this is the members tend to assume that when a new member unites with that congregation they have consummated that sale. The contents of this volume are based on the premise that frequently it is easier to become a member of a Protestant congregation than it is to be accepted into the fellowship of that community of believers.

One result of these institutional pressures is to encourage church leaders to place the highest priority on selecting members to staff the business positions and committees of the congregation. A lower priority often is given to staffing ministry committees such as an evangelism committee or a board that is responsible for the assimilation of new members. In some congregations these committees are not staffed or do not function. By contrast, the trustees and finance committees often are two of the best staffed and most active committees. This may represent a drift away from evangelical Christianity and toward cultural religion.

Another result of institutionalism is a lack of clarity on the definition of what constitutes church growth. For some it is simply gross numerical growth, regardless of the source of the new members. For others, it is growth by conversions only. For a few it is growth in the quality of the spiritual life of the members.

The tenth assumption is that every congregation has a system for reaching, receiving, accepting, and assimilating new adult members. In many congregations this is a very passive system and consists simply of receiving adults who walk in on their own initiative and ask to unite with that congregation. In other congregations the basic system is to delegate the entire responsibility to the pastor. The thesis of this book is that it is better to have a broader-based, more active and more intentional system. For many congregations this will require changing the current system. The normal response to innovation or change from within an organization is to resist it, to explain why that will not work here, to change the agenda to legalistic issues, to shift the discussion to another subject, to suggest postponing the subject to another time, to ask for another meeting, or to defend the present system. These are the kinds of responses anyone should expect who seeks to change the present congregational system for receiving and assimilating new members. A better approach is to recognize the price of growth and prepare to pay the price.

Finally, it is assumed that one of the most effective pedagogical models is to encourage the individual to reflect on his or her own experiences. There is an intentional effort to present the material contained in this volume in a manner or style that will encourage the reader to reflect on what is happening in the reader's congregation, to reflect on and order the reader's own experience, and to challenge the reader's own assumptions on this subject.

I am grateful to the thousands of lay persons, pastors, and denominational staff members I have met in parish consultations, workshops, seminars, and retreats who have stimulated my thinking on this subject. They have enriched me with hundreds of insights and scores of illustrations on the subject of reaching and assimilating new members. This volume represents an expression of my gratitude to them.

I
What's the Glue?

"We've lost our sense of unity," exclaimed a member at Bethel Church. "When I was a youngster this was one big happy family. Well, maybe we weren't always happy, but we certainly were a lot more unified than we are today. It seems that ever since Pastor Krueger left back in 1972 we've been going downhill."

"Well, I'm kind of new here," declared a man who had transferred his membership to Bethel fewer than two years earlier, "but I've been in a half dozen different congregations since my wife and I were married and I'm convinced a church does its best when it has a mortgage. Give the people a challenge and they'll respond. When a congregation doesn't have a challenge, that church flounders."

"I think we were at our strongest back in the late 1950s," reflected another person in the group. "That was when we were heavily involved in camping and outdoor recreation here at Bethel. A little over twenty-years ago we received a gift of that ten-acre wooded parcel of land on the west side of town. We developed that into a summer camp area, built the retreat center, and began having an early worship service there every Sunday in July and August. I bet at least two-thirds of our members worked on that project. We had a work crew out there nearly every Saturday for three summers plus a lot of Saturdays during the rest of the year. My wife and I were talking about that the other night. Every one of our closest friends today is a person or couple we really got acquainted with while we were working out there at Bethel in the Woods. This congregation hasn't been as closely knit since we finished the retreat center out there back in the early 1960s."

"You have to remember that over one-half of today's members have joined Bethel since we finished developing that camp site," offered another member. "Although they use it and enjoy it, none of them have had the experience you and I had in going out and spending twelve or fourteen hours a day doing the work in developing it. That was a unifying experience for those of us who were here then, but you have to realize we're only a minority out of the 450 people who are confirmed members of this congregation today."

"I guess you're right," came the response, "but we sure were a lot more unified as a congregation back in those days than we are today. Developing that camp was a part of the glue that held this congregation together for a long time."

What Is the Question?

This conversation illustrates an issue that affects every middle-sized and large congregation. Some are more acutely aware of it than others. It rarely comes up for open discussion except when the members are conscious of a lack of cohesiveness or unity in the parish. This is one of the most important, but frequently overlooked factors in both he assimilation of new members and the rejection of potential members.

Every long-established congregation is organized around one or more principles which weld a loose collection of individuals into a cohesive group. Once a congregation passes the 35 to 50 mark in worship attendance, this glue becomes an important factor in understanding the distinctive characteristics of each congregation. As time passes one form of glue is often replaced by a new organizing principle which rallies people together and unites—or reunites—them as one fellowship. Whenever one of these components referred to as glue disappears, either it is replaced or that congregation begins to diminish in vitality, enthusiasm, size, and outreach.

Once a congregation passes the 50 to 65 level in worship attendance, one or both of two patterns begin to emerge. In some congregations the ratio of participation to size begins to decline as the membership figure climbs. The larger that membership total, the lower the ratio of worship attendance to membership. In other congregations this pattern is at least partially offset by one or more forces that tend to increase the cohesiveness of the group. When the congregation reaches the 70 to 100 level in worship attendance, it usually is very helpful to examine the sources of this sense of unity. It is even more important to consider this factor when a congregation begins to decline in outreach and size.

In addition to the variable of size, a second consideration necessary to understand this concept is the distinction between a commitment to Jesus Christ as Lord and Savior and a commitment to one particular congregation. The first does not necessarily generate the second of these two loyalties, and this distinction can be seen very clearly in scores of churches where there is no reason to question the Christian commitment of members, but many of them clearly do not feel a strong sense of belonging to that particular parish.

The congregation with twenty or thirty or forty members is small enough that it can be glued together by the two great commandments of Jesus—the love of the Lord and the love of the members for one another. By contrast, however, the congregation with two hundred or more members usually is far too large and much too complex to function as a "large small group." The sense of unity needs additional reinforcement as the size of the congregation increases.

Another way of stating this is to ask the question, What is the basic organizing principle that holds a congregation together? Answering this question often will throw some light on concerns about the participation or lack of involvement of the members. There are at least a score of different organizing principles which often help to glue together the parish with more than thirty or forty members, although it should be understood these are not mutually exclusive. One of these organizing principles may be very influential in reinforcing the loyalty of some members to that congregation but may be of no significance for other members. Likewise some members may be tied to that particular congregation by two or three components of the glue which keep potential members from joining. As one organizing principle fades away in terms of encouraging a sense of unity, it may be replaced by two or three others. For some people what are described here as separate principles may have a high degree of overlap while for other members one principle may have tremendous influence and have no overlap with others that appear to be related to it.

A Checklist for Self-Evaluation

You may want to ask yourself which of these organizing principles used to be a part of the glue that held your congregation together. Which ones no longer are very influential? Which ones are the strongest cohesive forces today? What does this checklist say to the sense of unity in our church today? If the nature of the basic organizing principles has changed during the past several years, what are the implications of that change? If a very important piece of the glue has disappeared recently, what has been developed to replace it?

1. The nationality or ethnic-language factor.

Perhaps the clearest example of a single influential organizing principle in the history of Christianity on the North American continent has been the nationality church. Close to one-half of all the Roman Catholic parishes in the United States today were first organized as Irish or German or Slovak or Bohemian or Polish or some other nationality parish.

The same pattern was repeated with thousands of

24

Norwegian or Swedish or German or Finnish or Danish Lutheran parishes. The nationality tie was *the* basic organizing principle in these congregations. That element of the glue can still be seen in Christian Reformed congregations in Iowa or Michigan filled with Hollanders or the German Reformed churches in eastern Pennsylvania or the German Mennonite congregations in western Canada.

Lest anyone see this as an obsolete principle it should be added that there are thousands of recently organized Spanish, Samoan, Haitian, Japanese, Chinese, Korean, Greek, Filipino, Vietnamese, and Latvian congregations in the United States today, most of them less than twenty years old. Several denominations, led by the Southern Baptist Convention, are actively and aggressively organizing new congregations today with language, nationality, race, or ethnic ties as a basic organizing principle.

2. The denominational identity.

This has been a very strong factor in many congregations from several denominations including the Lutheran Church-Missouri Synod, the Episcopal Church, The Presbyterian Church in the U.S., the Christian Reformed Church, the Amish, and the Cumberland Presbyterian Church. It is a factor of decreasing influence in most large mainline Protestant denominations and is of declining influence in those denominations which are the product of recent mergers. It varies greatly as a factor among the congregations in such denominational families as the Southern Baptist Convention, the Lutheran Church in America, the Christian Church (Disciples of Christ), and the United Presbyterian Church in the U.S.A. In some denominations, such as the Baptist General Conference, the Christian Reformed Church, and the North American Baptists, the combination of nationality, background, and denominational identity produces a strong unifying influence.

3. The personality and magnetism of the minister.

In many congregations the most important single organizing principle is the attractive personality of the minister.

25

This can be seen clearly in many large independent congregations, in new missions, and in long pastorates. Sometimes members believe the personality of their minister is what holds the congregation together. Other members say the glue is in the minister's sermons. And still others cite long tenure as the reason the minister is such a cohesive force.

The obvious difficulty is what happens when that minister dies, retires, moves, or is incapacitated? The usual result is either (a) a sharp decline in the congregation or (b) replacement with either another magnetic personality or with other cohesive forces.

(4) A specific, attainable, measurable, highly visible, and unifying task.

A building program is the most obvious example of this organizational principle at work in a congregation. Another common example is paying off the mortgage. Less common is the congregation that is unified around the responsibility for the financial support of a missionary in a foreign country. In each case, however, that specific goal has become a significant cohesive force.

(5.) The kinfolk ties.

In some congregations fifteen or twenty members are related to one another through blood or marriage, another fifteen or twenty are related to a second family, and a third family tree accounts for another eight to twelve members from two or three or four households. When two or three family trees dominate the membership of a congregation, their influence often can be divisive. When there are a half-dozen or more family clusters in a congregation, it may be a very healthy part of the glue and a major positive element in the internal communication system of that congregation.

(6. The enemy.

One of the most widely used organizing principles employed in transforming a loose collection of individuals into a tightly knit and cohesive group is to organize "against the enemy." It has been widely used for centuries; and it is used in community organization, war, business, labor unions, and the church. One illustration of this principle is in a popular history of American Methodism, *Organizing to Beat the Devil,* by Charles W. Ferguson (Doubleday, 1971). Many of the large "independent" churches of today were originally developed using this principle. It is widely used by those seeking to lead a congregation out of the denomination. Without realizing it, this principle often is used by a youth minister or a youth director to organize a collection of young persons into a cohesive group. The "enemy" chosen frequently when this principle is used to develop a cohesive youth group is (a) the senior minister or (b) the parents or (c) the schools or (d) society.

The use of this organizing principle as a cohesive force was illustrated several years ago by a group of Episcopalians who were very dissatisfied with the rector of that downtown parish. Rather than create an unpleasant situation they quietly organized nearly one hundred members into a group which initiated the proposal to start a new mission on the north edge of the city. The dislike for the rector was the primary organizing principle that brought that group together, and the vision of a new mission was a distant second. After they had been meeting together in temporary facilities for several weeks, the bishop of that diocese met with them to announce the name of the priest who would be assigned to that new mission—the clergyman who had been serving as the rector of the downtown parish which they had left.

Another application of the same principle, which can be seen with considerable frequency, is the group of members who appear to have little in common, but band together into a tightly knit, very active, and extremely cohesive group to force the resignation of the pastor. When they have accomplished their objective, the glue that held the group together evaporates very quickly, and it is not unusual for several of them to drop into inactivity or to leave the congregation within several months after the arrival of the next minister.

In other congregations the satisfactions that accompany membership in such a closely knit and cohesive group are so great that the members soon organize against the new minister.

The widespread use of this principle is one of the most persuasive, pragmatic proofs of the validity of the doctrine of original sin.

7. Social class.

Scores of congregations bear a distinctive community image as "the status church" or "the prestigious congregation of this denomination in the city" or "where you'll find the doctors, lawyers, judges, and other community leaders." This frequently is a very strong and self-reinforcing cohesive influence in "Old First Church Downtown." It tends to be seen most often in Episcopal, Presbyterian, Baptist, and Methodist congregations.

The struggle to keep the doors open or to maintain the separate and distinctive identity of "our church" often is the most influential organizing principle today in (a) many small congregations, (b) the long-established congregation that once was a large and prestigious church and now is only a fraction of its former size, and (c) the congregation that has been dominated for decades by one family.

8. The crisis.

Perhaps the best illustration of this component of the glue can be found in those congregations that have seen their meeting place destroyed by a fire or a tornado or a hurricane or have seen a flood fill the church building with several feet of dirty water and scores of dead fish. The almost inevitable reaction is a rallying together by the members to respond to that crisis. Old divisions are overlooked, and the congregation becomes a remarkably unified and cohesive group as they work on the highly visible common task (see item 4 above) and respond to the urgency of the crisis.

In Pennsylvania one congregation was contemplating

dissolution when Hurricane Agnes struck in June 1972 and filled the basement with flood water which rose to nearly six feet in the sanctuary. As the members worked together to clean out their meeting place, the crisis eliminated the discussions on dissolution. Who could vote to dissolve such a tightly knit fellowship of committed people?

There are three elements to the sequel following the crisis which should be recognized here. First, the new adult members who unite with such a congregation a few months before the crisis hits and who are deeply involved in responding to the crisis find they are very quickly accepted, assimilated, and taken into the family. Several months after the crisis has passed they are absolutely convinced this is a very open, warm, receptive, loving, and easy-to-enter congregation. They cannot comprehend why anyone would describe it as "cliquish" or "closed" or "cold." Second, the new member who moves into the community several months after the crisis has passed and the property has been restored or rebuilt often feels like the only homesteader among a group of pioneers. He finds it very difficult to be accepted and assimilated into the life of the fellowship circle because he has no firsthand recollection of the disaster which is a shared experience for everyone else. Finally, the pastor who lives through the crisis with the members often develops a very close and mutually supportive fellowship with the people there. After a move to another congregation that minister frequently is disenchanted with the lack of this close, caring, and supportive fellowship in the new congregation and soon is ready to move on again.

9. The group life.

Thousands of congregations are intentionally organized around the development of a large and ever-growing number of small face-to-face groups such as Bible study groups, adult Sunday school classes, circles in the women's organization, youth groups, prayer circles, recreational teams, hobby groups, and mission task forces.

This is one of the healthiest and most productive

organizing principles on this list. It is widely used in rapidly growing and strongly evangelistic urban churches. The larger the congregation and the more central this organizing principle is in the life of that congregation, the more essential it is that the church be adequately staffed to nurture, reinforce, and maintain the group life.

The congregation organized around this principle will require more staff than the same size congregation organized around a common nationality background or against the enemy or the magnetic personality of the minister, but it is worth that additional cost. This is one reason that, as the ethnic and nationality glue erodes, it becomes necessary for the large Swedish or German or Norwegian heritage congregation to increase the size of the staff when the twenty-year pastorate comes to an end.

10. Community building.

Occasionally a congregation undertakes a task in which the most significant results are the building or reinforcing of a sense of community among the participants, and the task itself is of secondary, long-term significance.

The development of a camp and retreat center by the Bethel Church described earlier is an example of community building as an organizing principle. That experience also illustrates that what was a very central part of the glue in one era of a congregation's history may be an irrelevant factor for the members who joined after the end of that era.

Another example of the use of community building as an organizing principle is the use of the five- or six-day canoe trip to weld the members of a confirmation class of young teen-agers into a caring and supportive fellowship.

William P. Janssen, minister of the Burch Presbyterian Church of Fort St. John in British Columbia, led a group of young people on a 182-mile, six-day rafting trip from Fort St. John to the town of Peace River. In an eleven-minute, color slide review of that experience, Mr. Janssen notes that "at one point the raft trip passed for three days through isolated wilderness before encountering the first signs of civil life—an isolated farm. To celebrate this break from isolation we visited the aged bachelor occupant to learn that he was a Presbyterian Christian longing for fellowship." He added "campfire times were terriffic—times of singing and sharing, of relating how Jesus could change our lives, and had—in many ways—in some of us."

The community-building principle is one of the most creative methods of turning a collection of unrelated individuals into a closely knit fellowship. Jesus used it with the men we refer to as the Apostles.

11. Theological stance.

In perhaps 10 to 20 percent of all Protestant congregations, the dominant organizing principle is based on the position of that congregation on the theological spectrum. "This is the most conservative church in town" or "This is the only liberal church in town" are the words often used to articulate this operational principle in organizing a congregation into a cohesive and unified group. There is unity in conformity. (It is worth noting that the first Christian Church council, Acts 15:1-19, was called to decide whether the unity of the church would be in conformity or in Jesus Christ.) This basic organizational principle has limited value except in those congregations which perceive themselves as being at one end or the other of the theological spectrum and is far more significant as a cohesive force in the extremely conservative congregations than for those at the liberal end of that spectrum. Rarely is it a significant factor for the congregations in the middle 80 percent of the spectrum. Some observers contend this is a very basic principle for church growth. They contend that the theologically pluralistic congregation is unlikely to be a growing congregation.

12. Program and ministry.

Those congregations which are not at either extreme of the theological spectrum usually find it very difficult to use "We are a middle-of-the-road, orthodox, Christian congregation" as an organizing principle. Instead they may glue the parish together with one or two or three specialities in ministry such

31

as the following: the best music program of any church in this community—the only weekday Christian day school—the greatest community ministry of any church in the city—the strongest missions emphasis of any church in the association—the most energetic evangelism program—the biggest Sunday school in the city—the only church with a comprehensive ministry to single parents—the best counseling program in the country.

This organizing principle ranks with the emphasis on the group life of the congregation as two of the healthiest forms of glue that a church can use to weld a large collection of individuals into a cohesive and unified congregation. In both cases, however, one price tag is a larger-than-average program staff. Another price tag is a major emphasis on creativity and innovation in responding to the needs of a passing parade of people.

13. Place and building.

For many long-established and dwindling congregations the members' attachment to *this place* often is a major part of the glue that binds that group of people together. This clearly is a major component in holding together the congregation that is closely tied to a cemetery or the congregation that places at the top of the priority list the maintenance of "this beautiful building."

Like any other heritage tie, this organizing principle has very little attractiveness in reaching the unchurched or newcomers to the community, but it may be very, very influential in causing longtime members to maintain their affiliation with and participation in the same congregation, despite a move to a new residence six or ten or fifteen miles from the meeting place.

14. Heritage and nostalgia.

The denominational and congregational heritages combined with a nostalgic longing for the good old days often help strengthen the sense of congregational cohesion in many long-established churches. The members of the typical congregation where heritage and nostalgia are major cohesive forces often describe the "recent new members" as people who have joined since 1960 and the "young members" as those under fifty years of age.

15. Growing old together.

For one reason or another many congregations continued to receive new members and to assimilate them into the life of the fellowship circles of the parish up through the early 1950s. Beginning sometime during the 1950s, however, these congregations gradually lost their ability to attract and assimilate new people. Today the strongest single cohesive factor in those churches is that many of the members have been together in the same parish for two decades or more. "All of my friends are here" or "When we joined, this was a congregation of young couples with small children; now we are a congregation of middle-aged people with relatively few children at home" are often-heard expressions of this organizational principle.

The typical congregation in which this is a major component of the glue today usually will display two or three of these characteristics: (a) the median tenure date for today's members is at least fifteen years—in other words, one-half of today's members joined this congregation at least fifteen years ago; (b) for every husband-wife couple with children under age eighteen at home, there are at least two couples who do not have children under eighteen at home (if the congregation was representative of a cross section of the American population, these two family types would be approximately equal in number); (c) the median age of the adult (age eighteen and over) membership is above fifty years of age (for the American population it is forty-three years); (d) at least 15 percent of the adult members are widowed (in the American population this figure is approximately 9 percent); (e) most of the adult, new members who have joined during the past decade either had friends or relatives in the congregation before joining or possess an above-average ability to build friendships with strangers; (f) less than 10 percent of today's leaders united

33

with this congregation during the past three years; and (g) at least one-half of the members live beyond a mile from the church building, and two-thirds of the leaders live at least two or three miles away.

In those congregations where growing old together is an especially significant cohesive force there often is a reluctance to recognize the strengths and assets of the congregation such as a meaningful ministry to persons born before 1925 and strong pressures to "reach more young families." In part, this stance may represent a desire to turn back the calendar, in part it may represent a fear that if the congregation does not reach more young families the church will close, and in part it may represent a negative reaction to the normal processes of aging. Frequently this creates a climate for a problem-based approach to planning and produces more frustrations than would a potentialities-oriented planning model.

16. The church secretary.

In some congregations, and especially those with a comparatively high turnover rate among the ordained staff, the church secretary with fifteen or twenty or more years of service may be a very significant unifying force. This is more frequently true when the secretary is strongly person centered (as contrasted with the task-oriented individual), acts as the communications hub for that church, and takes a tremendous interest in all facets of parish life.

Occasionally, but far less frequently, the "career associate minister" who serves the same congregation for a decade or longer or the popular choir director or the extremely personable custodian or the friendly church business manager serves as a significant cohesive factor, but that is less common than to see the church secretary acting as a vital part of the total glue.

17. The liturgy.

In some congregations, such as the Anglo-Catholic parish in a "low church" Episcopal diocese, the liturgy is the most

34

distinctive unifying force. Although it may not be as influential, this same form of glue occasionally is found in the highly liturgical Lutheran, United Methodist, Presbyterian, Baptist (yes, Baptist!), or United Church of Canada congregation.

18. The congregational life-style.

An increasing number, but still a very tiny proportion, of congregations, have developed a distinctive participatory, celebrative, and relational style of congregational life and worship. In many of these congregations this has become the central organizing principle that glues that collection of individuals into a remarkably cohesive group. This appears to be increasing in several denominational families including Presbyterian, Lutheran, Methodist, and Episcopal.

19. Organizational structure.

In dozens of congregations the governing board (consistory, session, council, etc.) has a role, a history, a tradition, and a responsibility that makes it stand out as the dominant cohesive force in that congregation. An excellent example of this was the consistory in many Christian Reformed congregations in the 1930s, 1940s, 1950s, and 1960s or the session in several Presbyterian congregations in the 1960s or the voters' assembly in several Lutheran Church-Missouri Synod parishes or the vestry in many Episcopal parishes.

20. The choir director.

The long tenure, full-time choir director who has served with a series of relatively short term pastorates, and who has developed a music program with several choirs, may be a strong unifying force.

This list is intended to be illustrative, not exhaustive. Readers may be able to identify other organizing principles which are significant cohesive forces in other congregations. In some congregations, for example, the charter members provide a continuing cohesive force, and it would not be difficult to add others to the list.

The Exclusionary Glue

Far more important than building a complete list of all possible organizing principles in unifying a large collection of individual church members is a different question: Which of these organizing principles, which of these cohesive forces, which of these unifying factors tend to cause potential members to feel excluded? One side of the picture is that the factors described here tend to reinforce the individual commitment of various members to *this* congregation. The glue helps to explain why some members may move their place of residence five or ten or twenty miles and continue to drive back to the old church. The glue helps to explain why some families continue in the same congregation for three or four generations despite a scattering of the individuals. The glue helps to explain why some congregations attract certain "church shoppers" who visit other congregations and keep on shopping until they find *this* church. The glue helps to explain the continued loyalty of certain members who display considerable discontent with certain phases of the church program or are unhappy with a particular staff member.

The other side of that picture is that the glue can become gummy and begin to cause some people to feel excluded. Perhaps the clearest examples of this can be seen in the English-speaking people who do not feel welcome at the Korean-language church; or the person who married into a church dominated by one or two family trees; or the blue-collar worker who comes to an upper-class church which places a premium on excellence in verbal skills; or the new arrival who visits the congregation that has just completed the restoration of the building following the flood of three years ago; or the theological liberal who walks in on a theologically conservative church; or the person who prefers the relatively passive, traditional, and highly liturgical worship experience who attends the worship service at the church down the street which features an informal, participatory, and celebrative worship service; or the twenty-seven-year-old husband and his twenty-five-year-old childless wife who wander into a congregation that proclaims itself as a family church, but where the leadership is drawn largely from persons born before 1925 who have been members there for at least twenty-five years, and the dominant glue is growing old together. In general, the stronger the inclusive and cohesive factors, the more likely the average visitor will not feel welcome.

Questions for Self-Examination

1. Which forms of glue have been the most influential cohesive and unifying factors in your congregation in past years?

2. Which ones are no longer present or much less influential than they were in previous years?

3. What has been the impact of the disappearance or decline of some components of the glue?

4. What new cohesive and unifying factors have been added in recent years to replace some of the glue that has disappeared?

5. What are the five strongest and most cohesive forces in your congregation today? Rank them in order of influence.

6. Which of the five may tend to cause visitors and potential members to feel unwelcome here?

7. What could be added to the current list of cohesive and unifying forces that would (a) strengthen the loyalty, commitment, and involvement of the present members and (b) cause visitors and new members to feel welcome here?

II
Whom Do We Exclude?

"I was reared an Episcopalian," reflected Bill Armas as he responded to the question on why he was a member of the Clearview Church. "My wife comes from a strong Lutheran family. We met while we were in college, but neither one of us was attending church at the time. We were married in the Lutheran Church where my wife was a member, but we pretty much dropped out of church after we were married. Several years later I started drinking too much, and the next thing I knew I was an alcoholic. Finally, my wife persuaded me to attend an Alcoholics Anonymous meeting, and I accepted the fact I am an alcoholic. I dried out and haven't touched a drop for over eight years now, but I know I'm still an alcoholic. Shortly after I went on the wagon we found we needed to go to church. Since I still considered myself an Episcopalian, I went and talked with the rector of an Episcopalian parish not far from where we live. When I asked what he served at communion he replied that they used wine, but assured me it wouldn't hurt me. I knew better since I know I am an alcoholic. So we visited a Lutheran church, and after we had been there a few Sundays, I saw they served only wine at communion. I explained my problem to the pastor, but he said it was all in the head and the wine wouldn't hurt me. My wife and I know I cannot touch a drop of fermented beverage so that's why we're here. This church serves grape juice at communion, and I know I am safe here."

"My wife's arthritis got so bad that she could hardly climb the five steps to get into the sanctuary," explained Tony

Cepek, "but she insisted that we continue at First Church. We had joined there back in 1933, and most of our friends are there; but when they moved her Sunday school class from the first floor parlor to the second floor, she agreed we should come out here where everything is on one floor. It was a very difficult decision to make, but that's why we're members here. Now that we've been here awhile, we've made some new friends, and we like it here more every Sunday."

"Our story is probably the most unusual one here," suggested Wayne Page when it came his turn to explain why they were members of the Clearview Church. "As you all can see we're an interracial couple. After Helen and I were married, we tried going to a couple of black churches, one of which is the church I grew up in as a boy, but the women there treated my wife like dirt. I guess they felt she was unfairly using up what is a scarce commodity in the black community. Next we visited several white churches, but in each one some of the white men made no secret of how they felt about a white woman marrying a black man. Let me tell you, it got a bit rough in two of them. So we just dropped out of church for over a year; and then we heard through some friends that this congregation included two interracial couples, so we thought we would give it a try. We've had such a warm welcome that we've been here ever since. That's our story."

"We're here because this is the only church we know that has Sunday school classes for visually handicapped children," explained Sally Mitchell, a forty-year-old mother of three. "My husband and I both grew up in the same denomination. We met in a church college and stayed in that same denomination until five years ago. Our second son, who is now nine years old, is nearly blind, and we switched our membership to this church when we found it had three special Sunday school classes for the visually handicapped. Our denomination apparently doesn't recognize the existence of such handicaps."

"My husband has to work on Sunday morning about

forty-eight Sundays a year," observed Mary Bouton as she responded to the question of why she was a member of this church. "That didn't bother us particularly since neither one of us ever had been members of a church. Two years ago, however, when we first accepted Jesus Christ as Lord and Savior, we began looking for a church that had a regular worship service on other than Sunday morning. We started coming to the seven o'clock Thursday evening service, liked the people we met, and decided that if this church cared enough to offer a special worship service for those who have to work on Sunday morning, this must be where God wants us to be. I guess we're the only ones in this group this evening who are Thursday night regulars, but my husband has his vacation coming up next month, so we'll see you on Sunday morning at least once or twice next month."

"I take more convincing than some of you," began the thirty-one-year-old John Fletcher as he gripped the arms of his wheelchair to shift his body slightly. "I've been in this wheelchair ever since I had an automobile accident in 1968. I've always called myself a Christian, and I've been a regular church attender as far back as I can remember. After I got out of the hospital and was able to get around in a wheelchair, I decided I was not going to give up going to church. The first Sunday I went to church back home, I cried like a baby. Our men's club had built a special ramp so I could wheel myself up into the sanctuary. It was their surprise gift to welcome me back to church. For the next several years I rarely missed worship, and that ramp got its share of use. I usually sat in a side aisle in the sanctuary for worship. When Anne and I moved here, we began to look for a church and our first Sunday here I knew this was it because you were expecting me. Since this building is all on one floor, we don't need a ramp. What caught our attention and made us know we were welcome is the pew arrangement. Instead of having a pew all across the back on each side, there is a short stub of a pew on the aisle at both ends, and the space between is for wheelchairs. Anne sits in a two-person pew with our six-year-old son. I sit to her left, next to me is Mrs. McCoy in her wheelchair, and Mr. McCoy sits in the short pew next to his wife. We both can sit next to our spouses, and we're protected from someone walking around the corner too sharply and bumping into our wheelchairs. This is only the second congregation I've ever seen that really expects people in wheelchairs to attend worship. So, in answer to the question as to why we're members here, we're here because it appears that people in wheelchairs are expected."

How many of these new adult members of the Clearview Church would feel equally welcome in your congregation? Or would some of them feel some sense of exclusion? Before going into greater detail on this issue of exclusion, it may be useful to review another example of how congregations have the freedom to make people feel excluded or make them feel welcome.

"Next Sunday I'll go outside to receive a severely crippled woman into membership," explained the Reverend Russell C. Lee as he pointed to the glass wall on the east side of the chancel at Faith Lutheran Church in Albuquerque. "That's really a glass door in the middle of the wall, and I can step through there and go out into the parking lot where I will receive this lady into membership here. She is crippled so badly that she could not come into the sanctuary, but she can get into a car, and she and her husband are here almost every Sunday for our drive-in service. Actually," continued this very creative pastor, "we do not have a special drive-in service. Our congregation is simply seated in different places. One group sits on the left side of the aisle, a second group sits on the right side of the aisle, a third group sits in the choir section, and a fourth group sits in their cars in the parking lot. . . ."

"Our summer is a little shorter than Albuquerque's," commented the Reverend Don Salberg of Trinity Lutheran Church in Yankton, South Dakota, "so our drive-in service runs from the end of May to the first Sunday in September. We have several individuals, couples, and families who rarely miss a Sunday during the summer. Several are physically handicapped, some are probably scared away by our building, and I suspect others simply cannot endure crowds. There are many people, you know, who find it very difficult psychologically to be in a crowd of people. Our drive-in service gives these people an opportunity to participate in corporate worship that otherwise would not be possible."

"We started our drive-in worship service fifteen years ago," observed a layman who had spearheaded the effort at Bethel Church to offer this alternative worship service. "We've kept it going despite the indifference of one minister and the opposition of a second, but now we have the vigorous support of our present pastor. When we remodeled our sixty-year-old building, we decided that rather than provide a big sanctuary that would be filled only two or three times a year, we would use our parking lot for our overflow. Once we started," he continued, "we found that a lot of people who had never attended before started coming. We usually have anywhere from ten to sixty cars with people in them during the church service."

"What has surprised me," added another layman from Bethel, "is that a lot of older people and invalids appreciate the chance to come to a funeral service and stay in their cars. We still have a lot of funerals here at the church, and I've seen many a time when we had three hundred people in the sanctuary and another two hundred outside in cars for the funeral of someone who had lived here a long time and had a lot of friends."

"Some of our members thought that a drive-in worship service was a possibility only in Florida or southern California," commented a third layman from the same congregation, "but people are comfortable out here seven or eight months out of the year. From May through September, two-thirds of our visitors worship out here in the parking lot rather than inside the church. I guess some of them feel you have to dress up to come to church, but you can worship in your car in the same clothes you wear to the beach or on a picnic or to a ballgame."

"I was pretty much opposed to it when the idea was first brought up," confessed a fifth man from Bethel, "especially when our pastor didn't give us any support. But now as I look back on our experiences I can see several advantages.

"First, of course," he continued, "we're reaching a lot of people with the Word that we never reached before. Second, we're accommodating several handicapped people who found it very difficult to get to church before. Several of these are our own members who had just about dropped into inactivity, but most of them are people we had never seen before. Third, our total attendance is up about 40 percent from what it used to be, and at least half of that is the result of the drive-in alternative. Fourth, a lot of the newcomers to this community shop around for a while before they pick a church. Our drive-in service makes it real easy for people to come here to look us over. They don't feel trapped like a visitor sometimes feels when he can't get out of church until he's promised to join that congregation. When they're in their automobiles people feel like they're on their own turf. They're more comfortable. Fifth, it's the cheapest overflow space we could possibly build. I've seen those churches that will seat 800, but on 45 Sundays out of the year they have fewer than 150, and it gives a sense of defeat rather than victory and joy to the worship service. Here our pews are comfortably filled on most Sundays of the year, but we can accommodate twice that many more out in the parking lot if we have to for one reason or another.

"Finally," he concluded, "this has been the best thing that ever happened to our men's club. Our men's club was on its last legs fifteen years ago when we decided that we would sponsor the drive-in alternative. We bought the original sound equipment, and four years ago we replaced it with this low-power radio transmitter so people can hear the service on their car radios. We have a dozen men out here every Sunday from March to November. We greet the people, serve them doughnuts, orange juice, and coffee right in their cars. We have a bunch of trays that fit over the car window, just like the drive-in restaurants. Several of our men call on people who visit here, and every year several of the new members of our church are people we first met out here in the parking lot. In fact, the current president of our men's club first got acquainted with our church when he and his family began coming here for the drive-in service."

Before dismissing the idea of a drive-in or boat-in worship service as completely irrelevant to your situation, it might be helpful to look at the widely practiced alternatives. Some congregations stay with the same Sunday morning schedule twelve months a year and accept as a fact of life the summer slump. Tens of thousands of congregations with steep steps up into the sanctuary assume that when a person is no longer able to climb those steps that person should stay home. Apparently they would prefer to encourage these members to stay home or to attend another church rather than offer the alternative of a drive-in worship service.

While the "informed estimates" vary widely, apparently there are at least one million adults in the United States and Canada who psychologically are unable to mingle with the crowds and therefore have to stay away from the traditional church service. These people are victims of agoraphobia, the fear of public places and crowds. Often they are reluctant to leave home. When they are forced to mingle with groups of people or to be in a crowded situation, they are subject to sudden attacks of panic. The symptoms of these attacks include shortness of breath, dizziness, dry mouth, trembling, pounding heart beats, sweating, a sense of weakness in the legs, confusion, and the fear that one is dying. After one or two of these attacks the person is very, very reluctant to mingle in crowds. If your community has a population of 25,000, the chances are that there are 125 to 250 of these people living in your community, and four-fifths of them are women. The regular drive-in worship service allows these people to share in the corporate worship of God.

In many other congregations it is widely assumed that the person recovering from an illness or an accident should not expect to be able to participate in corporate worship until completely recovered. Other congregations have a comparatively strict, although informal, dress code which causes some members to stay away during the hot summer months.

In evaluating the alternative of a drive-in or a boat-in worship experience, the appropriate question is not, Should we consider this possibility? A better question is, What are we doing or not doing now that causes some people to stay away from our worship services, and would a drive-in worship service eliminate some of those reasons?

Now, with that introduction to the subject, it may be appropriate to shift the scene to an informal discussion late one Friday evening. About a dozen of the thirty-five people who had gathered for a weekend workshop on church planning were sitting around discussing common concerns after the formal session had adjourned.

"What do you mean, whom do we exclude?" asked Mary Chandler in an indignant tone of voice. "At Wesley United Methodist Church we don't exclude anyone. Everyone who accepts Jesus Christ as Lord and Savior is welcome. Our church is an open church; we don't exclude anybody."

"I can remember when we excluded anyone who spoke only English," reflected sixty-eight-year-old David Knutson of Messiah Lutheran Church. "Our parish was founded as a Norwegian Lutheran Church in 1884, and until the middle 1920s everything was in Norwegian. Our constitution was translated into English in 1925. In 1926 we began to use English in the worship service for the first time. Today, however, we welcome everyone."

"Exclude may be too strong a word for our situation," commented Barbara Anderson, "but when my mother came to visit us I discovered we certainly discourage anyone who is unusually sensitive to the glare from spotlights from coming back. When the new sanctuary was constructed at First Baptist Church, the architect designed the lighting system to use a large number of spotlights. The fixtures are beautiful, but there is a lot of glare. My mother's eyes are very sensitive to bright lights, and there are only three places in the sanctuary where she can sit without getting a headache from the glare."

"Do any of you sign the worship service?" asked Frank Newman of Westminster Presbyterian Church. "If we don't have someone translating the worship service into sign language, it seems to me that we're excluding the deaf."

"I never thought of that," replied Mrs. Chandler. "We certainly don't think of ourselves as excluding anyone, but I guess a deaf person would not feel welcome at Wesley."

"The only people we exclude from membership," declared Jim Martin from First Christian Church, "are the persons who have been baptized by sprinking or pouring and refuse to be baptized by immersion. We're a closed membership church, and we do exclude some people who would transfer their letter of membership if we were an open membership church. We see it most clearly by the fact that when one of our young members marries a Methodist or Lutheran or Presbyterian or Episcopalian the person from our congregation usually ends up changing denominations and going to the spouse's church. Except for that, we don't exclude anyone, except maybe the deaf."

"I hadn't thought of it quite this way before," observed Mary Andrews from the Second United Church of Christ, "but I guess we exclude anyone from worshiping with us if they can't climb about two dozen steps. Our sanctuary is on the second floor, and it is quite a climb. I guess you could say we exclude the lame and the crippled without realizing it."

"We talked about building a ramp up to the main entrance at our church," explained John Luchek from St. Paul's Episcopal Church, "but then we realized that wouldn't help much. Once you're inside the building you still have to go either up or down steps to get from one part to another. I guess we are pretty effective in excluding people in wheelchairs."

"When this discussion began, I thought you were going to talk about how middle-class, white churches exclude blacks, the poor, and the needy," interrupted Bob Marelli. "How come no one's mentioned that?"

"I don't like this word 'exclude.' I think that's much too strong," declared Nancy Becker who had been silent to this point. "I've been sitting and seething inside. I don't understand how people who call themselves Christians can sit and talk about a church excluding anyone who wants to come and worship God. I simply cannot believe that any of us exclude people from our churches."

"You're suggesting that exclude is an active verb, if I understand your feelings correctly," responded Barbara Anderson. "I feel much as you do, Nancy, and I kind of recoiled when we first began this discussion using that word. It does make it sound as if we're intentionally keeping people out of churches. What we're really talking about is a more passive stance. We don't actively exclude people, we simply fail to do those things that would make more people feel welcome."

"Now wait a minute!" exclaimed Bob Marelli. "Don't tell me that white churches have not actively excluded blacks. We all know that racial discrimination in the churches has been the result of an active stance by white people. There's been nothing passive about that."

"I think we're talking about both the active forms of exclusion and also the more numerous forms of passive exclusion," responded Frank Newman. "My hunch is the passive forms of exclusion are far more common."

"Let me give you an example of what I am convinced is an innocent and passive form of exclusion," offered Barbara Anderson. "I've become a close friend of a woman who moved here several months after her husband had died. Last week she confided in me that she almost dropped out after coming to our church for a few weeks. She said that although she had been widowed only a few months when she moved here, she was treated as though she had always been a widow. Without our realizing what we were doing, we were making a distinction between our support for the woman who was widowed after she and her husband had been members here for many years and the woman who came to our church after her husband, whom we had never known, had died. In effect, she said we had an exclusionary policy against women who came to our church after being widowed. This came as quite a shock to me."

"I've been sitting here building a list of people we exclude from our church back home," reflected Chuck Peterson. "To begin with, we exclude anyone who cannot read or understand the English language, people who do not care for a highly liturgical worship service, those who cannot climb stairs, the deaf, the blind, persons in wheelchairs, people who prefer grape juice rather than wine for Holy Communion, those who cannot tolerate poor preaching, and those who cannot afford the quality and style clothes our members wear. We exclude these and many others without ever realizing that we are in fact an exclusionary parish. I must confess I had never thought of it in these terms myself until tonight."

"Whether we do it actively or passively, we do exclude many people from our churches," declared Frank Newman. "Maybe we can help our people back home understand what we're talking about if we take them a list of some of the people we exclude or fail to make welcome or do not accommodate. I think it would be a useful exercise to try and build a list of the categories of people who would not feel welcome in our churches back home."

Questions for Self-Examination

1. Whom do you exclude? Who are the persons who might not feel welcome or comfortable or at ease in your congregation? (It may be most helpful to go over this list with the membership and/or evangelism committee of your congregation.) Check each category of persons who might feel unwelcome.

Non-English Speaking People

Black Americans

American Indians

Puerto Ricans

People Who Cannot Climb Stairs

The Deaf and Those with Hearing Disabilities

Koreans*

Filipinos*

Chinese*

The Visually Handicapped

The Mentally Retarded or Mentally Ill

Mexican Americans

Persons in Wheelchairs

Women Who Were Widowed Before Coming to Our Church

Childless Couples

Single Parents

Unmarried Couples Living Together

Those Who Would Not Be Comfortable with Our Order of Worship

Alcoholics

Non-Christians

The Extremely Shy or Timid Persons

People Who Feel They Cannot Dress Suitably for Our Church

Single Adults, Especially Single Male Adults

People Whose Eyes Are Sensitive to Glare

Parents Seeking a Church That Has Sunday School for Young Children at the Same Hour as Worship for Adults

Post-High-School-Age Youth

Teen-agers

Divorced Persons

Persons Who Are Divorced and Remarried

Those Opposed to Ordination of Women

Those Favoring Ordination of Women

Those Who Work on Sunday Morning

Radical Dissenters

The Very Wealthy

Homosexuals

Anyone Who Is Very Nervous in Crowds (Agoraphobic)

Anyone Who Feels "Lost" in a Large and Complex Building

Illiterates

Hippies

"Jesus Freaks"

The Very Poor

---

*In recent years the number of immigrants to the United States from Korea, China, and the Philippines (combined) has been nearly as large as the total immigration from all of Europe.

Couples and Children of an Interracial Marriage

Persons with a Low Level of Competence in Verbal Skills

Drug Addicts

Persons Who Are Physically Disfigured

Persons Not from This Denominational Family

2. Can you add other persons to this list?

3. Of the groups you have checked who might not feel welcome here, which ones are you intentionally discouraging or excluding?

4. Of the groups who probably would not feel welcome or "at home" here under the present circumstances, identify the ones you would most like to make feel welcome here. Select only two or three categories. What must you do to change the situation so these people would feel welcome? Who has the basic authority or responsibility in this congregation for making these changes? Who should approach them about making these changes?

5. Now, go over the list one more time and focus your attention on the categories of people you did not check as those who would not feel welcome here. These are the ones you decided probably would not feel excluded and might even feel welcome here. For each of these categories identify the program, group, special event, or other reason you believe these people would feel welcome in your church. Be specific!

III
Twelve Ways to Keep People from Joining Your Church

"Why are you a member of *this* parish?" asked the denominational staff member of each of a dozen individuals who were gathered to talk with him about the evangelistic outreach of Trinity Church.

"My wife was a member here, and so I joined when we were married ten years ago," was the first response.

"I guess I was born into this parish," replied the next person in the group. "Both of my parents have been members here since before they were married."

"We just walked in," explained a third member of the group. "My husband and I both have been in this denomination all our lives, and since this is within easy walking distance of our house, we simply started coming here the first Sunday we were in town."

"Well, I've been coming here for over twenty years," responded Jeff Reynolds who appeared to be in his middle forties, "but I didn't become a member until last winter when our new minister, Pastor Johnson, came and called on me and invited me to join."

"You just became a member last winter!" exclaimed a woman sitting across the table from Mr. Reynolds. "Why, Jeff, I thought you had always been a member here. I know I've been seeing you around Trinity ever since my husband and I moved here, and that's close to twenty years ago. How come you didn't actually become a member until last winter?"

"Nobody had ever asked me to join," replied Jeff Reynolds in a quiet voice.

Don't Invite Them

This incident illustrates one of the most widely used techniques to keep people from joining the church. Do not invite them to unite with "our church." While this may sound unbelievable to many parish leaders, some people do operate on the assumption that they are not welcome unless they have been invited. While they may drop in for worship without an invitation, they may not return unless they have been made to feel welcome, and they are unlikely to indicate any interest in uniting with this congregation until after an invitation has been extended by a member.

Today church growth is emerging as a top priority in many denominations and in thousands of congregations. Much has been written on how to encourage church growth and on the recruitment of new members. Workshops are being offered all across the country to train both the clergy and laity in the skills necessary to develop a growing church.

These are important issues, and they deserve the attention they are receiving, but the emergence of this high priority on church growth has obscured another related and very important skill that has been developed to a very high level of competence in thousands of congregations. This is the skill of discouraging church growth and the ability to discourage potential members from uniting with the church. Many congregations have spent ten, twenty, or even thirty years practicing several of these skills and have perfected them to the point that practically no "outsiders" with the possible exceptions of several people who got in by marrying a member and a handful of extroverted, aggressive, and very personable individuals who completely ignored the efforts to exclude them, have joined these congregations since the late 1950s or early 1960s. Church leaders who are interested in church growth, the evangelistic outreach of the parish, and the assimilation of new members, as well as those who believe "our parish is already too large," may find it instructive to review several of these techniques and skills.

Several of these are even more subtle than the glue and the exclusionary principles described in the first two chapters. Unless they are identified and eliminated, they will tend to seriously inhibit potential church growth.

As described earlier, the most widely used technique to keep people from joining is not to invite them. This skill includes not inviting people who are not actively involved in the life of any worshiping congregation as well as the church shoppers who visit your church on Sunday morning, friends, neighbors, and people who associate with your members at work or in the various facets of community life.

The Impact of Short Pastorates

A second technique that is widely used, especially by many smaller congregations, to keep people from joining is to change ministers every two or three or four years. This is one of the most effective means of preventing church growth. Countless studies have demonstrated very clearly that pastoral leadership is a critical factor in church growth. In its report to the 1976 General Assembly of the United Presbyterian Church the Special Committee on Church Membership Trends declared, "Growing congregations . . . are characterized by stronger pastoral leadership," and "The Church . . . must adequately recognize strong pastoral competence as a decisive factor for the vitality and outreach of a congregation."

One of the means of reducing the positive impact of pastoral leadership is to change ministers every few years. Why is this true? First, there is overwhelmingly persuasive evidence that *from a long-term congregational* perspective, the most productive years of a pastorate seldom *begin* before the fourth or fifth or sixth year of a minister's tenure in that congregation. Thus by changing pastors every two or three years a congregation has an excellent chance of avoiding those most productive years. While there are exceptions to this generalization, and the productive years of some pastorates do begin with the first or second year, these are sufficiently rare that a congregation usually can depend on avoiding the problems that result from rapid growth by changing ministers every few years.

A second reason that this is usually a reliable means of keeping people from joining your church is the natural response to the arrival of a new minister. Again there are exceptions to this generalization, but most congregations greet the newly arrived minister with a passive stance.[1]

We assume you brought your program with you, Pastor.—The first year of a new pastorate should be spent getting acquainted and building the trust level.—Go ahead, Pastor, and develop your program for this congregation and then tell us what you want us to do.

These are some of the statements that are frequently used to describe that first year. Each of them has a built-in acceptance of a passive stance by the members. This passivity often is reinforced by the various forms of grief over the departure of the predecessor. Some members may spend the first year of a new minister's tenure grieving over the predecessor's departure, deciding whether or not they want to risk all the hurt that accompanies the loss of a close friend by building friendship ties with the new minister, and by watching to discover what radical changes the new minister may suggest.

When a congregation has had only one or two ministers stay longer than four years since before World War I this passivity often reappears if and when a minister reaches the fourth year of his tenure in that congregation. Everyone knows the pastor soon will be moving on to greater challenges.

A passive congregation rarely attracts new members. Thus by changing ministers every two or three years a congrega-

---

[1]For an elaboration of this concept and suggestions on how a minister can respond creatively to this passivity see Lyle E. Schaller, "Getting the Most Out of the Honeymoon," *Christian Ministry,* May 1977, pp. 29-33.

tion can regularly practice its skills of passivity and thus not encourage new people to unite with that church.

Perhaps the most important reason that changing ministers frequently is an effective means of discouraging church growth is that increasingly life is being perceived as primarily relational. If one takes a purely functional view of the role of the minister it is easy to justify short pastorates. From this perspective the emphasis is on what the minister does, not who he or she is. At least 85 percent of the lay people in the typical congregation tend to think primarily in relational, not functional terms, however.[2] When this is coupled with the assumption that a basic characteristic of a growing church is that the members are enthusiastic about their faith, their church, and their minister (see Preface, assumption 7), it becomes apparent that one way to prevent church growth is to encourage a frequent change in pastors. It is difficult for most lay persons to be consistently enthusiastic about their church and their pastor if there is a change in ministers every two or three years.

Finally, dozens of surveys have demonstrated that rapidly growing congregations tend to be churches with long pastorates, and stable or declining congregations tend to have short pastorates. While these surveys do not prove a direct cause-and-effect relationship, the statistical relationship is sufficient that changing ministers frequently is one of the most effective means of keeping people from joining your congregation.

The Impact of Financial Subsidies

A third technique for reducing church growth has been tested and proved in literally hundreds of congregations from many different denominations. This is to provide a substantial *long-term* financial subsidy from the denomination. This technique has been used widely with new missions

---

[2]For more detailed discussion of this concept see Lyle E. Schaller, *Understanding Tomorrow* (Nashville: Abingdon, 1976), pp. 38-45.

out in suburbia, with long-established inner city churches, and with congregations in changing or transitional communities. Frequently it is necessary for the denomination to subsidize these ministries at a critical stage in their development. Usually the short-term financial subsidy, if continued only for a period of one to four years, does not have a major negative impact on church growth. When this subsidy is continued for several additional years, however, it frequently helps to create or to reinforce conditions which tend to discourage church growth. One condition is the "welfare syndrome" or sense of dependency. Another is low morale. A third is a low level of congregational self-esteem. Another is passivity. A fifth is a sense of powerlessness or lack of control over the destiny of the congregation. A sixth is a fostering of the belief that a larger subsidy and more money will solve all problems. Another is focusing attention on the congregation-denomination relationship rather than on an evangelistic outreach.

This pattern can be seen very clearly by contrasting the relatively large financial subsidies provided The United Methodist Church or the United Presbyterian Church to its home mission projects with the relatively modest financial subsidies provided by the Southern Baptist Convention to its new home missions and examining the growth rates of these missions. Within specific denominational families the congregations that have been receiving a long-term denominational subsidy frequently have a significantly slower growth rate than similar congregations that have not had the "benefit" of a long-term denominational subsidy.

Criteria for Evaluating Potential

A fourth technique for keeping people from joining your church is to keep the focus on real estate when discussing how many more members a congregation can accommodate. Unquestionably the most common example of this is the debate over whether a congregation should change its schedule to include two worship services on Sunday morning or to continue with one. (Sometimes the actual question is to change from two back to one, but the basic issue is the same.) "Why should we change to two services when we never fill the sanctuary for one service?" is a common response to a proposal to offer people a choice of two worship experiences on Sunday morning. Without going into detail on the advantages and disadvantages of two services, this comment illustrates the tendency to use physical space as the basic criterion for determining whether a congregation can accommodate more members.

The result of this chain of reasoning is that there are literally thousands of churches where the leaders are baffled when the congregation fails to attract more new members and to grow in numbers. After all, there is plenty of room for more people at worship, there are several Sunday school classes which could easily accommodate double or triple the current attendance, and there may even be empty rooms which could be used for new classes. Why does this congregation not attract more people and grow?

While this response does not apply to all such cases, there are at least three reasons why some of these congregations with many empty or half empty rooms do not attract new members.

The most common reason is that the church is under-programmed. The size, scope, and variety of the program is adequate to accommodate only the current number of members. Closely related is the fact that many of these congregations with an excess of physical space are under-staffed. The current number of program staff members may have been adequate when the congregation was composed of a more homogeneous collection of individuals and when several other components of the glue (see chapter 1), which are now absent, were present to help weld this large collection of people into a cohesive and unified congregation. For today's conditions, however, the congregation is now understaffed.[3] A third reason that many of these congregations, which appear to have room to grow, do not succeed in reaching many new members is the limited range of choices offered to people. In an age when the culture is encouraging people to express their individuality and to expect a range of choices, many congregations insist on offering people only three basic choices, (a) take what we offer, (b) stay home, or (c) go somewhere else.

Thus one tried and tested method of keeping people from joining your church is to focus the discussion on building space when the question arises as to whether or not this congregation is prepared to grow. The larger the building facilities, the more effective is this technique!

The Impact of Architectural Evangelism

What appears to be the opposite of this last factor is actually a fifth technique that has been widely used as a means of keeping potential members away. This can frequently be found in the many congregations which either have relocated from a former downtown site to a new and promising location out in a residential area and/or the congregation founded in the 1950s or early 1960s. In each case the plans called for construction of a very large facility for corporate worship. For example, if the congregation was averaging 185 at worship with a peak of 300 on Easter, the new sanctuary was planned to seat 500 or 600. "If you build a large, beautiful, and worshipful sanctuary, people will be standing in line to get in when it is completed" was the promise implied in the vision of what could be if only people had more faith in the future and in their leaders.

Eventually the new building is completed, and the attendance at Sunday morning worship now averages 175. The members come together every Sunday morning to

---

[3]For a discussion on adequately staffing a congregation, see Lyle E. Schaller, *Survival Tactics in the Parish*, (Nashville: Abingdon, 1977), pp. 176-78.

celebrate the resurrection of Jesus Christ and experience a psychological defeat as two-thirds of the seats are empty. In simple terms, one very effective means of keeping your church from growing is to place your trust in architectural evangelism rather than in person-to-person evangelism.

The Impact of Self-Image

Closely related to these last two procedures is a sixth approach that has been used by thousands of congregations to avoid the challenges and changes that usually accompany church growth. This is to perpetuate the small-church self-image. This technique requires the leaders to identify their congregation as a small church and to function as what Carl Dudley has described as a "single-cell church."[4] This means the congregation functions as one large small group. Instead of seeing this as a congregation of groups, organizations, classes, circles, task forces, boards, committees, departments, and individuals, the leaders perceive it as a congregation of individuals and try to operate on the premise that it is one large circle or cell. Usually the congregation is too large to function as a healthy small group, and thus it is in effect a supersaturated solution with more members than can be absorbed into one group. These congregations usually are able to assimilate replacement members to take the place of members who move away, drop out, or die; but rarely are they able to grow. Church growth becomes possible only if and when these churches change from a single-cell to a multi-cell style of congregational life. Thus a very effective means of keeping potential members from uniting with your church is to function as a single-cell small church. This technique has been used with many congregations which have as many as four hundred to five hundred members.

---

[4]For an elaboration of this syndrome see Carl S. Dudley, *Making the Small Church Effective* (Nashville: Abingdon, 1978).

The Impact of Intercongregational Cooperation

While this seventh approach to avoiding church growth runs counter to the natural inclinations of many people, including this writer, there is an increasing accumulation of evidence that church growth and intercongregational cooperation are incompatible goals.[5] Or to state it very bluntly, the congregations that are receiving an unusually large number of new members tend to be the churches that are not actively involved in intercongregational cooperative ministries. This is a descriptive statement of how the world appears to be, not a value judgment of how it should be.

To discuss why this appears to be the dominant pattern means moving this discussion from the descriptive level to the level of speculation, but there appear to be at least seven responses to the question, Why? First, congregations with a high level of self-esteem, where the members are enthusiastic about their church and where there is a clear identity of role and purpose (three common characteristics of growing churches), rarely participate in cooperative ministries. Second, the time and energy of both the clergy and laity that are devoted to the cooperative ministry often means that much less time and energy is available for reaching unchurched people. Third, cooperative ministries rarely have a strong, overt evangelistic dimension. Fourth, for any one of the participating congregations to place a major emphasis on reaching prospective members through the cooperative program might appear to be unfair to others and therefore often is de-emphasized. Fifth, by its nature a cooperative ministry tends to de-emphasize the distinctive assets, strengths, program, and ministry of the participating congregations and to highlight the ministry of this inter-congregation effort—and people unite with congregations,

---

[5]For a provocative discussion of this basic point from another perspective, see C. Peter Wagner, *Your Church Can Grow* (Glendale: Regal, 1976).

not with cooperative ministries. Sixth, some of the leaders, both lay and clergy, become so enthusiastic about the cooperative ministry that they fail to communicate to people outside any church an equal enthusiasm for what is happening in their own congregation. Finally, and perhaps most significant, there are some responsibilities that can be accomplished most effectively by an intercongregational approach and some that can be accomplished best by a unilateral approach. Issue-centered ministries, the theological education of the next generation of ministers, and administration of a pension system for church employees fit into the first category. Corporate worship, maintenance of a meeting place for the worshiping congregation, Sunday school, and evangelism usually can be accomplished most effectively by a unilaterial approach. *Key 73* demonstrated that an effective effort in evangelism can be implemented only by individual congregations, not by a cooperative approach. So, if you want to keep your church from being bothered by a lot of people wanting to join, place a heavy emphasis on intercongregational cooperation.

The Impact of the Cutback Syndrome

An eighth widely used approach to avoid church growth can be described very simply by the term cutback syndrome. This is reflected in such frequently heard comments as these:

Last year we combined the two evening circles in our women's organization into one.—We are in the process of merging two of our adult Sunday school classes.—The attendance at our first worship service on Sunday morning has dropped to an average of thirty-five, so we have cutback to just one worship service.—So few young people were coming that we combined our junior high youth group with the senior high group.—We decided the best way to increase our choir membership was to combine the youth choir with the adult choir.—We tried going to two worship services on Sunday morning for a year; and while our total attendance increased, it seemed to many of us that we were dividing the church and creating two

61

congregations, so we have gone back to only one service.—We felt our teachers deserved a vacation so we cut out Sunday school for the summer.

These comments illustrate some of the many facets of the cutback syndrome. There are at least five major reasons why this is one of the most effective means of discouraging church growth. First, by reducing the number of groups in the church, this reduces the opportunities for new members to find a place of entrance, acceptance, and fellowship. Second, the more sensitive any organization is to the needs of people, the more complex and diverse its organizational structure. By reducing the complexity of the congregational program structure, that church becomes less able to be sensitive and responsive to the diverse needs of people outside any worshiping congregation. Third, a reduction in the organizational and program structure reduces the need for additional leaders and workers. Thus the old-timers can carry the load. New members are not needed and do not feel a sense of being needed. Fourth, by reducing the range of choices available to members, the range of events and experiences to which members could invite non-members is reduced. Finally, expectations do influence performance. Adoption of the cutback motif tends to create a self-perpetuating cycle which largely eliminates the possibilities for church growth.

The Transfer of Responsibility

The ninth technique on this list is probably the easiest of any to implement, and it usually works. It can be summed up in the often-repeated observation: "We're here every Sunday morning at the same time; if they are interested they should be able to take the initiative. The doors are wide open. If they want to come to church, all they have to do is walk in, and they'll find we'll welcome them." The "they" variously refers to people who are not active in the life of any worshiping congregation, to newcomers to the community, and to anyone who might be described as a prospective member.

It is difficult to reconcile this position with Matthew 28:19, but it is easy to equate it with the doctrine of original sin, and it is one of the more effectve methods for keeping people from joining your church.

Subversion of the Agenda

A tenth technique that often has proved to be a useful means of preventing church growth is somewhat more difficult to describe because it comes in many different disguises and frequently is not easily recognized. In general terms it can be described as shifting the focus of the congregational agenda from ministry to institutional mainte-nance. The means to an end becomes an end in itself and crowds the basic purpose of the church off the agenda.

A comparatively highly visible example of this is the congregation which launches a major visitation-evangelism effort because more members are needed to help raise the money necessary to repair the roof. Equally effective, perhaps more common but less visible, is the decision to maintain the status quo for the next several years so the present pastor can finish his ministerial career here without any disturbances or intrusions before retiring. A third example is placing the top priority in the allocation of resources on the maintenance of the meeting place. A fourth example is the congregation that reduces the program staff in order to pay for a building renovation effort that must be completed before the one-hundredth anniversary of the founding of that congregation.

The Impact of the Literalists

Another technique to keep your congregation from being overwhelmed by new members can be illustrated by two congregations, both of which place a heavy emphasis on visitation evangelism. The procedure at the first church was explained in these words:

> We try to call on every new family in the community within ten days after they move here. Our callers have been trained to be able to identify the good prospects in one visit. In that first call we try to identify the needs of that family and to match them with the appropriate group or class or organization in our church. If they don't respond to that call, we write them off. If they're interested in the church, they'll respond. If they're not interested, there's nothing we can do by continuing to call on them.

This congregation reached its peak in size in 1953 and has been on the decline ever since, although the rate of decline has been slowed since they began this visitation-evangelism program in 1971.

Slightly more than a mile away is the meeting place of another congregation of the same denomination. The lay volunteer in charge of their visitation program described it in these words:

> Our goal is to have one or two of our members call on every newcomer to this community within ten days after they move here. The primary purpose of that first call or two is to build a relationship between our members and the newcomers. With a few rare exceptions we never even consider whether we should continue calling on the newcomers until after we have completed seven or eight calls at that home. Many of our most active members said no when we first invited them to our church. Our building is so large and so impressive that it tends to scare a lot of people away. Besides that, most of the people moving in here are working-class people and they tend to see us, partly because of our building and partly because of our history, as a prestigious, upper-class church. We interpret those first two or three negative responses as meaning, *not-yes, now*. We can't afford to take a no literally!

This congregation peaked at 1800 members in the early 1950s, dropped to less than 300 in 1968, and now includes more than 900 members, most of them recent newcomers to that community.

In other words, an effective way to keep your church from growing is to interpret that first No literally. (This also is an effective means of increasing the proportion of new members who will drop into activity. For details, see chapter 7.)

Rifle or Shotgun?

"How can you suggest that we focus our evangelistic efforts on any one group?" asked Mrs. Robert Burton with a mixture of surprise, disappointment, bewilderment, and exasperation in her voice. "That would not be Christian! We welcome everyone here. To ask us to concentrate on any one group would be discriminatory, and as Christians we can't discriminate among God's children."

This response confuses two very different operational questions and also raises a very basic doctrinal question on the nature of the church. The first operational question is, Do we welcome everyone who wants to worship with us? Mrs. Burton was correct in her contention that as a Christian congregation we have no alternative but to welcome everyone who accepts Jesus Christ as Lord and Savior. The second operational question is, Who are the people we are trying to reach with our evangelistic outreach? No one congregation can reach and minister to everyone. The English-speaking congregation will have difficulty trying to reach and serve persons who speak only Korean or individuals who speak only Swedish and prefer to worship God in their native tongue. The congregation which meets in a building with many different sets of stairs will have difficulty in reaching people who find it hard to climb stairs. The research coming out of the Church Growth Movement suggests very clearly that the easiest (but not the only) way for a church to grow is to focus its evangelistic outreach on a narrowly and precisely defined segment of the populaton.[6]

---

[6]For a full description and defense of the concept of the "homogeneous unit" in church growth, see C. Peter Wagner, *Our Kind of People: The Ethical Dimension of Church Growth in America* (Richmond: John Knox Press, 1978).

Whether one completely accepts this basic concept of church growth or not is largely irrelevant to this discussion. At a minimum, however, it is important to recognize that the most effective beginning point for any congregation seeking to reach people who are outside any worshiping congregation is to focus on one precisely defined segment of the population, identify their specific needs, mobilize the resources necessary to be able to respond to these needs, and begin to build the relationship between the members and the people the congregation is seeking to reach. No one congregation has the resources necessary to respond to the needs of every unchurched person.

This raises the basic doctrinal question: In theological terms, how do you define the nature of your congregation? Do you see it as *the* church? Or do you see it as one institutional expression of the universal church? The universal church is expected to reach and minister to everyone in the name of Jesus Christ. That is an extravagant burden, however, to place on any one congregation. For example, the gospel is preached in Chicago in at least forty languages every week. That is necessary. Is it reasonable to believe that every Christian congregation in Chicago should preach the gospel in forty different languages every week? There is a difference between what God expects of his church and what he expects of each individual congregation. What piece of the total evangelistic responsibility of the church do you understand God has placed on your congregation? To answer, "All of it," is not only presumptuous, but also is likely to immobilize any congregation and to result in little happening of any significance.

To proclaim that "we are trying to reach all the people," probably means that you have adopted an effective technique for keeping people from joining your church.

Questions for Self-Examination

1. When is the last time you invited someone to unite with your congregation?

2. Review the list of adults who united with your congregation during the past two years. How many are children of members? How many came in via marriage to a member? How many came in on their own initiative? How many were invited by the pastor? How many were invited by another staff person? How many were invited by a member?

3. What has been the tenure for pastors in your congregation? Trace the records back to 1940. How many pastors stayed more than six years? How many moved before the beginning of their fifth year? Does this appear to have had any impact on the number of adults who united with your congregation *and were fully assimilated?*

4. When members of your congregation discuss the possibilities for church growth, do they tend to use building space as the basic criterion or do they use program, staff, and the group life as the criteria for determining whether your congregation could accommodate more people?

5. Is the Sunday morning schedule planned to offer people choices or to fill up the building?

6. Have you placed any emphasis on "architectural evangelism?" How has it worked?

7. Do the members see your congregation as a small church? Is it basically a single-cell congregation? Or is it a congregation of groups, classes, organizations, circles, committees, and individuals with very little overlap in the membership of the various groups?

8. What is the degree of involvement of your congregation in intercongregational cooperation? What has been the effect of this on church growth for all the participating congregations?

9. Have you been increasing and enlarging the number of groups, classes, organizations, choices, circles, and other small face-to-face groups in your congregation? Or have you been cutting back on the number? What has been the impact on church growth?

10. Do the members of your congregation actively accept

the responsibility for inviting people to come to your church? Or do you depend on unchurched people and newcomers to your community to exercise their own initiative and to come to your church without being invited?

11. Does the agenda at the typical board (or consistory or church council or session or vestry) meeting of your congregation consist largely of items of institutional maintenance? Or is the agenda dominated by ministry and outreach items? Check the actual agenda or the minutes for the last three meetings.

12. In inviting unchurched people to come to your church do your members tend to take that first no literally? Is there any system for repeated invitations?

13. What is your specialty, as a congregation, in ministry? What is the area of your greatest effectiveness in ministry? Are you attempting to build your evangelistic outreach on this strength or are you attempting to reach and to minister to everyone?

14. As you consider expanding the evangelistic outreach of your congregation, what do you see as the beginning point? Which segment of the unchurched population will you focus on first?

15. As you do this, which of the barriers to church growth described in this chapter will you have to eliminate? (At this point you may want to look more carefully at your congregation to identify other barriers to church growth. For suggestions on several other types of barriers to growth, see Lyle E. Schaller, *Survival Tactics in the Parish,* pp. 91-103, 135-43. Frequently a congregation finds it must identify and eliminate these barriers, most of which are not readily visible to the members, before it can launch an effective evangelistic outreach effort.)

IV
The Dynamics of Inclusion and Exclusion

The first three chapters of this volume have been devoted largely to identifying and describing several of the most neglected factors that are actual barriers in reaching and assimilating new members. Too often congregations, by their actions, attitudes, and traditions, tend to cause people to stay away completely or to cause the church-shoppers to continue looking elsewhere for a new church home. These first three chapters represent an attempt to sensitize church leaders to these barriers.

In this chapter the focus shifts to the dynamics of inclusion and exclusion. Perhaps the clearest method of presenting this concept is to look at a series of circles.

One means of illustrating the basic concept is to use two examples that may be found in the congregation with two full-time ordained ministers on the staff.

The background theory is that every congregation can be described in terms of two concentric circles. The larger outer circle is the membership circle. Every member is within that outer circle. The smaller inner circle includes the members who feel a sense of belonging and who feel fully accepted into the fellowship of that called-out community. Most of the leaders come from persons within this fellowship circle. By contrast, many of the workers who do not have policy-making authority, may

69

be drawn from among the members who are outside the fellowship circle. In some congregations workers may even be recruited from among the people who are outside the membership circle, some of whom identify with this congregation as constituents and some of whom are members of other congregations. One of the means of distinguishing between those within the fellowship circle and those outside it is the terminology; the former usually are comfortable with the pronouns we, us, and ours when referring to that congregation, while the latter tend to use they, them, and theirs more frequently.

The Dynamics of a Multiple Staff

The first example to illustrate how these circles can be used in describing the dynamics of inclusion and exclusion is a parish in which the pastor is now in his eleventh year as the senior minister. His first associate stayed three years and was followed by an associate minister who remained for four years. The third associate left after slightly less than two years, and the present associate arrived twenty months ago. In diagram 1, the relative positions of these two ministers is shown. The senior minister is clearly in the center of the fellowship circle. The recently arrived associate, who is now nearing the end of his second year, is out beyond the boundary of the fellowship circle. The associate, because of his location outside the fellowship circle, sees and hears things that are unknown to the senior minister. Some of the members, who also are outside the fellowship circle, feel much closer to the associate minister than they do to the senior minister. A few of them even turn to the associate for funerals or weddings rather than bother the senior minister. The senior minister, because of his presence at the heart of the fellowship circle, knows the board will never approve some of the proposals for change that the associate minister is suggesting. One of the reasons for what appears to be a communications gap between the senior minister and the associate minister is the difference in their perspective. The world looks very different to the person in the center of the fellowship circle than it does to the person outside that circle of intimacy. All three of the previous ministers moved before they ever were closer than the outer edge of that fellowship circle.

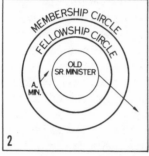

Diagram 2 is a picture of that same congregation taken three years later. The senior minister moved to another congregation a few weeks after the beginning of his twelfth year in this parish. That position was vacant for nearly a year while the church searched for a qualified successor. During that period the associate minister was the acting pastor, preached every Sunday, carried out all the responsibilities of the office of senior minister, and gradually moved into the fellowship circle. A month ago the new senior minister arrived on the scene. Since he is still a comparative stranger, and also is not as extroverted as his predecessor, he clearly is outside the inner circle. Within a year one of two things probably will happen. Either (a) the new senior minister moves into the fellowship circle and is fully accepted as a part of that inner circle, or (b) the associate minister resigns and moves away. The congregation cannot function effectively when the associate minister is in the fellowship circle and the senior pastor is outside that inner group.

The Recent New Members' Perspective

These circles also offer a useful method for discovering how new adult members feel about their acceptance in the congregation that they recently joined. On one occasion, diagram 3 was reproduced on a sheet of 8 1/2"x 11" paper and circulated as a part of a group interview with twenty-three

adults who had united with this particular congregation during the previous twelve months. The distinction between the membership circle and the fellowship circle was explained. In this explanation the additional comment was made that in most congregations, including this one, the fellowship circle actually consists of smaller circles. To symbolize this in a simple manner, two smaller circles had been added, each of which overlapped the inner and outer circles. The one on the left, for example, might represent an adult Sunday school class or a circle in the women's organization or a Bible study group which included people from both the inner fellowship circle and the outer membership circle. The small circle on the right might represent another group or team or committee or class drawing its members from both the inner and outer circles.

Each new member was asked to mark an X on the sheet to represent how well that person felt he or she was assimilated into that congregation. Placing an X just inside the outer membership circle line, for example, would indicate that the person making that mark felt a sense of membership, but that is all. An X halfway between the outer line and the line bounding the fellowship circle would indicate a feeling of some acceptance and a sense of belonging, but tempered with the recognition that that person was outside the inner circle. One young woman placed her X inside one of the smaller circles overlapping the fellowship circle, but outside the fellowship circle, and drew an arrow from that X to another X inside the fellowship circle to indicate that she felt she had been admitted into the fellowship circle by first joining a small group in the women's organization which included members from both inside and outside the fellowship circle. A husband and wife in their mid-forties each placed their X near the center of the fellowship circle to indicate that they felt fully accepted in this congregation—the fourth they had joined since they were married twenty years earlier. Five individuals placed their *Xs* directly on the line marking the outer boundary of the fellowship

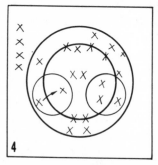

circle. After the sheet had been passed around and every new member had indicated his or her degree of a sense of acceptance or feeling of belonging, it resembled diagram 4 in this series of circles. When the person conducting the group interview saw the four *Xs* to the far left, he asked, "What do these mean? Did I explain it wrong? By definition everyone of you is within the membership circle." He was interrupted by one of the male new members who responded, "No, you explained it perfectly clearly. You said place an *X* where you feel you are. That's my *X* in the upper left-hand corner. While it is true that I am technically a member of this parish, I still feel like an outsider or a visitor or an intruder here, and you asked us to place an *X* where we feel we are in this assimilation process. That's my *X* well to the outside of the membership circle."

There are two morals on inclusion and exclusion in this story. First, it again illustrates a basic thesis of this book. In many congregations it is easier to become a member than it is to be accepted and made to feel so. Second, all four of the *Xs* to the left were placed there by husbands, suggesting that in this parish—as in many other congregations—there are more opportunities for wives to gain a sense of acceptance and belonging than are available to husbands.

Entrance into the Membership Circle

Before moving on to other facets of the dynamics of inclusion and exclusion it may be useful to examine how people come into membership in a specific congregation. For this purpose we use a diagram with only one circle—the membership circle. Everyone inside that circle is a member of the congregation represented by that circle.

When church members are asked, Why are you a member of *this* congregation rather than some other congregation in the community? most of the responses can be placed in the categories represented by diagram 5. (It should be under-

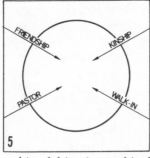

stood that this question is not addressed to the issue of why that person is a Christian but to the *primary* reason why that individual chose to unite with *this* congregation rather than with some other.)

The vast majority of persons offer explanations that can be classified under one of two terms —friendship ties or kinship ties.

When we moved here our neighbors were members of this parish, and they invited us to come with them.—My parents were both members here, and I have been coming since I was six years old.—My wife was born into this congregation, and when we were married I joined.—A friend at work invited us.—The first day we were in town the woman ahead of me in the checkout line at the supermarket began talking with me, and when she learned we had just moved here, she offered to come by on Sunday morning and pick us up. We've been coming back ever since. Between two-thirds and nine-tenths of the people give such responses.

Another 15 to 20 percent refer to the pastor as the primary reason, and 5 to 10 percent say, "We just walked in on our own," or offer some other reason such as the location of the meeting place or the name of the parish or the reputation of that congregation. Usually when pressed for more detail these "walk-ins" refer to denominational loyalty or location as the reason for walking in *here.*

Even more significant, friendship ties are mentioned far

more often in rapidly growing congregations than kinship ties. By contrast, in the declining parish, kinship ties account for a substantial number of all members while friendship ties are rarely mentioned. The smaller the number of recent new members—in proportion to the size of the parish—the larger the percentage of people who offer kinship ties, the pastor, the location, denominational ties, or just walked in as the primary reasons they are members.

This can be illustrated by looking at two similar congregations, each with approximately 400 active, confirmed members. During the past three years in the first church a total of 97 adults united with that congregation. When asked why they are members of *this* parish today, fourteen identified with the pastor as the primary reason, 57 pointed to friendship ties, 20 identified kinship ties (12 of the 20 married into this congregation), and the other six gave a variety of reasons. In the second congregation only 23 adults have joined during the past three years. When asked to explain why they are members of *this* parish today, 15 identified the pastor as the primary reason, two married into it, two listed other kinship ties, and four gave a variety of reasons. In this second congregation, the friendship lines apparently were almost completely inoperative.

The moral of this fifth diagram is clear. The congregation which seeks to grow should look at how friendship ties can be increased between individual members and those persons who are not active members of any worshiping congregation.

Four Routes to Inclusion

What happens to the adult who does not have any kinship ties to the members of that congregation recently joined? Which new members quickly gained a sense of acceptance and belonging? Which ones soon drop into a comparatively inactive role? Why? For some responses to those questions see diagram 6.

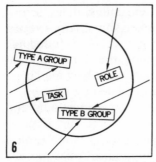

In the typical congregation, most new adult members fall into one of the five categories within a year of uniting with the parish.

The ones least likely to become inactive members are represented by the arrow pointing to the Type A group in this diagram. These are the individuals who become part of a group, where membership in that face-to-face small group is meaningful, *before* formally uniting with that congregation. They are assimilated before they join. One example of this is the man who comes down out of the choir loft in his robe to join the other new members standing in front of the chancel as they are being received into membership one Sunday morning. He had been assimilated into the choir before he formally joined that congregation. A second example is the woman who came into membership via a circle in the woman's organization. A third example is the couple who were invited by friends to attend an adult Sunday school class, they liked what they found there and subsequently joined that church. The distinctive characteristic of these groups is that membership is open to and includes people who are not yet formally members of that congregation.

Another group of new adult members is represented by the arrow pointing to the Type B group. These people become members of a group, where membership in that group is meaningful, *after* uniting with that congregation. They gain a sense of acceptance and belonging through membership in that smaller face-to-face group. This is an especially important part of the assimilation process in congregations with a hundred or more members where it is difficult for most newcomers to feel a real sense of acceptance except through participation in a subgroup of that congregation. Examples of these subgroups include the choir, a small group within the women's organization, a prayer group, the church council, a bowling team, an adult Sunday school class, a Bible study group, a men's fellowship group, a young adult group, a mutual support group, or a functional committee. The larger the congregation, the more important these small groups are in the assimilation of new members.

Other new adult members are assimilated by accepting a *role* or office which gives them a sense of belonging and causes them to identify with that congregation. This might be as a Sunday school teacher, counselor for a youth group, leader of a circle in the woman's organization, treasurer of a Sunday school class, usher, president of the men's group, trustee, or member of the governing body of that parish.

A fourth route that some new members take which helps them feel assimilated is to accept a *task* or job as a worker. These tasks usually do not have the formal status of an office and include such responsibilities as helping to clean the church on the first Saturday of every month, arranging for a coffee hour between Sunday school and worship, helping to count and package the Sunday morning offering, making telephone calls for the church, coming in one afternoon to help in preparing the weekly newsletter, helping in the kitchen for the monthly church suppers, or providing transportation for the youth group. These tasks may help the recent new member to gain a sense of acceptance and belonging and to begin to identify with that congregation.

The remainder of the new adult members do not fit into any of these four categories. Most of them either have or are in the process of dropping into comparative inactivity.

The moral of the sixth diagram is that adult new members who do not become part of a group, accept a leadership role, or become involved in a task during their first year tend to become inactive.

Assimilation and Commitment

The series of circles in diagram 7 represent an attempt to respond to the frequently asked question, Why aren't more our younger people and our newer members as committed as some of our old-timers?

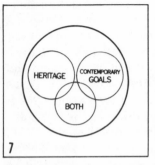

For purposes of analysis it may be helpful to distinguish between a commitment to Jesus Christ and a commitment to *this* parish. While it is impossible to defend this theologically, unless one turns to the doctrine of original sin, there are people who have a very strong commitment to Jesus Christ as Lord and Savior but are not involved in the life of any worshiping congregation. Likewise some skeptics contend that some of the most active church leaders have a very limited or very shallow Christian commitment. For descriptive and analytical purposes it may help to separate one's institutional loyalty to a specific congregation from one's Christian commitment. In this discussion the focus is on the loyalty or commitment of a member to a specific congregation and on the implications of this in the assimilation of new adult members.

In nearly every congregation there are members whose personal roots are closely interwoven with the roots of that parish. Examples of this are represented by these comments:

My grandfather helped build this church, or *I've been coming here since before I was born.—Both my wife and I are third-generation members of this parish.—My husband and I are charter members of this congregation.—My father was the minister here from 1937 to 1961.*

These shared roots, or this *heritage*, are the basis for that person's strong loyalty or commitment to *this* congregation. This heritage tie may be most obvious in those parishes that own cemeteries. It also can be seen in congregations which still carry a strong nationality heritage such as Swedish, Danish, Norwegian, Finnish, German, or Latvian. This heritage tie is also an important part of the commitment among the remaining charter members of the parish that was a new mission in 1949 or 1953 or 1963.

Another group of members feels a strong commitment or sense of loyalty to this congregation because of what it is doing in ministry and mission now. This sense of commitment through contemporary goals often has high visibility among members of the building committee as completion date for a major building program approaches. It also can be seen in the tie that binds Sunday church school teachers to the parish or in the commitment of a group of members to a specific mission program or outreach effort. This commitment also can be seen in the gratitude of the recently widowed member who discovers that this is a supportive community of Christians who do love one another. For some members the basic tie to that congregation is a personally meaningful worship experience week after week. These are the contemporary goals that hold their loyalty to that parish. A third and usually smaller group of members feel a sense of commitment to that parish through *both* heritage ties and contemporary goals. The members who do not fit into either categories tend to be the ones who do not feel a strong sense of commitment to *this* parish now.

The larger the proportion of members who feel a sense of commitment because of heritage ties and the smaller the proportion who are tied-in through contemporary goals, the more difficult it is to attract new members and the more likely it is that new members will soon lapse into inactivity. It is very difficult for new adult members, except perhaps for some of those who come into membership via the kinship route shown in diagram 5, to feel a sense of belonging or commitment to this congregation through the shared roots or heritage ties of institutional loyalty.

The moral of this seventh diagram is that since few new members can find a commitment through the heritage ties, the opportunity for new members to be involved in the contemporary goals of the congregation is critical in their assimilation into the fellowship of the parish. The congregations that have the best record on the assimilation of new adult members offer a variety of meaningful contemporary goals in which the new members can relate, support, and become involved in very easily and very quickly.

The Exclusionary Circle

From the perspective of the members of a congregation the most subtle of the ten circles described in this chapter is the wall that each congregation builds around itself. From the inside, from the perspective of the most active leaders, this wall does not appear to exist. Some deny their church is exclusionary. Others are aware of a few exclusionary characteristics but counter this with the declaration that "ours is a very friendly congregation. We welcome everyone." This feeling of openness and of a friendly posture toward strangers, visitors, and church-shoppers is reinforced by the comments of several recent, new adult members who feel fully accepted and who agree "this really is a friendly church."

There are three significant groups of people, however, that are missing from that congregational self-portrait. The first is composed of the newcomers to the community who visited that congregation once or twice and subsequently decided not to return. Their evaluative comments on the openness of that parish seldom are heard by its leaders. The second group is composed of the members who visited, joined, and later dropped into an inactive role. They found the exclusionary walls too difficult to penetrate. The third group is composed of those people who united with that congregation and subsequently, without changing their place of residence, transferred their membership to another congregation. Interviews with this group of ex-members yield different types of evaluative comments. These are seldom heard by the leaders of the congregation which they left. One of the fascinating dimensions of this third group is that many contend no one ever asked the question Why? when they stopped attending the church where they were members, began attending elsewhere, and later asked for a transfer of their membership. This apparent lack of concern or interest in what happened to them often reinforced their opinion that they made a wise decision in leaving that unfriendly congregation.

This exclusionary wall is illustrated in diagram 8 in this series of circles. It is the same pair of circles shown in the first

diagram at the beginning of this chapter, but this time the focus is on the height of that wall around the inner fellowship circle. From the perspective of the leaders, the long-time members and heritage-oriented people inside that inner circle, the line marking the boundary of the fellowship circle is no higher than the line painted on a gymnasium floor. Anyone who is interested and willing to take the initiative can step across it very easily and become a part of that inner circle. Some of the members of that inner circle go one step further and insist either that the line does not exist or that it is actually coterminous with the outer membership boundary.

A radically different picture is perceived, however, by the members who are outside that fellowship circle. Instead of a thin line painted on the floor, many of them perceive the boundary of that fellowship circle to be a circular masonary wall six feet thick and thirty feet high. They see a high, thick, and forbidding wall with several doors in it.

In one congregation, for example, this is what several recent, new adult members perceived when they looked at the boundary separating that inner fellowship circle from the rest of the membership. They saw one door in that circular wall labeled Young Married Couples with Small Children, and it was wide open. As one young couple in their mid-twenties approached that open door and started to go through it, they stopped and turned away because this was obviously not the door for them. Everyone in the group standing around talking just inside that door was at least forty-five or fifty years of age. A career woman in her early fifties who had never married found a door in that wall labeled Mature Women Who Have Never Married. She reported the door was not locked, but it took a lot of aggressiveness, self-assertiveness, and courage to push it open and enter a fellowship circle in which she was one of two women past thirty who had never married. Another door is labeled Mature Bachelors, but that was locked back in 1951 because of the fear that some mature bachelors might be homosexuals. Keys to that door, however, are readily available for any tenor who is willing to join the choir. A fourth door is marked For Timid, Shy, Bashful, Introverted, and Hesitant Individuals. That door is not locked and it swings open very easily, but the threshold of that door is four feet above the ground. The shy, timid, hesitant, and bashful members with limited self-confidence are reluctant to try to climb through that door for fear they may fall flat on their faces. Side-by-side can be found a pair of doors. One is labeled Workers and the other is marked Leaders. The first is unlocked and relatively easy to enter by anyone who is willing to assume the initiative, volunteer, and take orders. The second is guarded very carefully, and a person has to earn the right to pass through it—unless the member had a parent who was an active leader in that congregation, in which case, that member inherits the right to pass through the Leader door without showing any credentials. Another is labeled Divorced Persons, but it turns out that the only ones who gain easy admittance through that entrance to the fellowship circle are those who are divorced and remarried. A relatively narrow door carries the words, For Post-High School Youth, but the words are obscured by a hand lettered sign tacked to that door which declares Temporarily Closed: Come Back when You're Married and Have Two Children.

Some readers may be offended by this caricature of the exclusionary dimensions of the boundary around the fellowship circle. The purpose is not to offend but to encourage a critical analysis of the exclusionary characteristics of the fellowship circles of other congregations.

The Us–Them Syndrome

Another pair of circles that can be used by congregational leaders in evaluating the evangelistic outreach of their church and the congregation's ability to assimilate new members can best be illustrated by looking at diagram 9. One circle represents the members of the congregation. It is labeled Us. In this circle we list what "we" expect of ourselves in regard to reaching, receiving, and assimilating potential members of our congregation. In the second circle we indicate what "we" expect of the people who are not a part of any worshiping congregation.

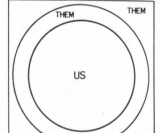

For example, in many congregations there is the expectation that newcomers to the community who are not a part of any local worshiping congregation will take the initiative in finding a new church home for themselves. *After* "they" take the initiative and visit our church, we will respond by contacting them. In other congregations there is the expectation they will find our meeting place, and they will take the initiative in asking to unite with "our" congregation. In some congregations, it is assumed that a visitor must attend worship at least twice before we are expected to respond to their initiative. In other congregations, it is expected that a visitor will fill out a pew card or call the church office if they desire a visit from a member or from the pastor.

In many of these congregations it is widely understood that "they"—the new members—must assume a major responsibility for gaining a sense of acceptance and belonging in this called-out community (see the last section of chapter 7 for a fail-safe approach to this assumption).

Perhaps the most divisive dimension of the us-them syndrome in the assimilation of new members can be found in the conflict over values and congregational life-styles. One example of this is an ex-rural congregation founded in 1903 which never included more than eighty members during the first six decades of its existence. In the mid-1960s, completion of an expressway encouraged scores of people employed in a large city forty miles to the west to move out to that attractive rural farming community in order to enjoy the combination of a city paycheck and country living. The rural congregation welcomed the first of the newcomers who began to attend worship in this open country church. Within five years the average attendance at worship had doubled from 33 to 65. One of the longtime members remarked, "It feels good to see the church filled week after week, and today we rarely hear the preacher talk about how we need to raise more money." After a few more years had passed, it became obvious that a new meeting place would have to be found. A four-acre site was purchased, but when it came to the decisive congregational meeting on approving a building program, the proposed relocation plan was defeated by a 68-59 vote.

• Subsequently one of the proponents of relocation calculated that the old-timers, persons who had joined this congregation before 1965, voted 41 to 13 against relocation. The newcomers, he reported, had favored the relocation plan by a 46 to 27 majority. "We had them outnumbered," he added, "but they were better organized and came closer to voting as a solid bloc than we did. If we wait and bring it up again next year and do a better job of getting our people organized, we should be able to win."

"If I had wanted to be part of a big church, I would have gone into town to church years ago," explained one of the longtime members, in describing his opposition to relocation. "We already have so many new people that I don't know everyone's name," declared another old-timer. "If they had succeeded in moving our church, in a few years we would have grown so much that I wouldn't know anybody." "We were a nice, friendly, small church until they moved out here," commented a person who had joined in 1946. "I don't object to their moving out here, after all, it's a free country; and I welcomed them when they started coming to our church. But why do they feel they have to change everything all at once?" "We had been doing all right at this site for over sixty years," agreed the leader of the opposition to the relocation proposal. "We had a good church and paid all our bills. Now they move out here and want us to borrow $150,000 to build a new building for them and their friends."

A second example is a new suburban congregation that was founded in 1958. The congregation grew slowly but consistently, and by the time the second minister left in the summer of 1971, the congregation was averaging 140 at the traditional service on Sunday morning, the mortgage on the second unit of the proposed three-stage building program was down to $18,000, and most of the leaders were thinking ahead to the day when they would build the permanent sanctuary. The third minister, however, came with a substantially different value system. He conceived of the church in terms of people, not buildings, and placed his major emphasis on strengthening the relationships among people and on improving the quality of interpersonal relationships. A year later he initiated the creation of a special worship task force which recommended adding another service to the Sunday morning schedule at 8:30 A.M. This Celebration of Life service was more informal, had a stronger orientation to family units, and placed a greater emphasis on active congregational participation than did the traditional liturgical service at 11 A.M.

Six years later the congregation appeared to have leveled off in size with an average attendance of 90 to 110 at the first service and 50 to 60 at the second traditional worship experience. Several of the longtime members had transferred their membership to other churches as an expression of their disapproval of the new direction that was being followed. These and other losses from the membership roll were more than offset by new families who had been attracted by the style of congregational life and by the new minister. Nearly all these new families attended the early worship service, while the congregation gathered for the second service was composed largely of longtime members who preferred the traditional format for worship.

By this time it did not matter what the subject of the conversation was focused on; it usually emphasized the differences between how "we" see the issue and what "they" prefer. The popularity of the pastor, the desirability of going ahead and completing the original building program, the optimum size for the congregation, the continuation of the Sunday morning schedule with two different worship experiences, the approach to Christian education, and the financial capabilities all elicited responses phrased in we-they terms.

This us-them or we-they syndrome arises repeatedly whenever the question of the assimilation of new members is discussed. In addition to the two examples cited here, it also appears when a congregation attempts to cross theological, nationality, linguistic, racial, social class, generational, educational, or sub-cultural lines in its evangelistic outreach to new members. It often has high visibility in any congregation with several members who are active in the charismatic renewal movement. Or, to use the frame of reference described in the first chapter, the "we" usually are glued into this congregation by a different combination of organizing principles than the "they" people.

Responses to Pluralism

How can a congregation respond creatively to this polarization as it seeks to reach and assimilate new members? How can this we-they division be minimized?

Unquestionably the easiest and the most widespread

response to the problem is to seek to reach only those unchurched people who come from that same narrow segment of the population spectrum as the members. What has come to be called "the homogeneous unit principle of church growth" is certainly the easiest approach to church growth. Long before it was formalized by researchers in the Church Growth Movement, this concept was intuitively acknowledged by church leaders who rationalized their evangelistic outreach by explaining, "They prefer to worship in their own churches." The referrent for the pronoun they might be persons from another nationality or language background, persons from a different social class, persons from another religious subculture, newcomers to the community, or any of several other distinctive segments of the population.

Another response can be found in the question, What is the basic source of unity in a congregation? Is it in conformity? Is it in Jesus Christ? Is it in a conformity of values, attitudes, behavior, dress, appearance, and customs that grow out of the same commitment to the same God and to the same Savior? This is a far more difficult question than first appears. Ever since the earliest days of the Christian church the leaders have been calling people together in councils to discuss the importance of conformity to right belief. From the Council of Jerusalem described in Acts 15:6-29 to Vatican II to the various contemporary denominational annual conventions on ordaining women, censoring seminary professors, and approving a new creed, church leaders have been meeting to talk about the differences between them and us and to decide on the criteria for keeping them out of our church.

A third response to pluralism has been to divide. One of the great examples of this was the Protestant Reformation of the sixteenth century. In parish terms, a church split has been a frequent response to diversity in congregational life. In the United States this was a very common response in the nineteenth century among Lutheran, Baptist, Christian, Mennonite, Church of Christ, Quaker, and Brethren congregations. Today, in the second half of the twentieth century, it is not uncommon although economically it is comparatively expensive. Sometimes the split has been caused by the younger English-speaking members of a German-speaking congregation, in other churches the division has seen the members of the charismatic renewal movement leave, and sometimes the split has seen the theologically conservative members walk out to form a new congregation.

This response to pluralism also can be seen today in many denominational families including the Presbyterian Church in the U.S., the United Presbyterian Church in the U.S.A., The Lutheran Church—Missouri Synod, and others.

Far and away the most common example of this response to the challenge of pluralism can be found in the thousands of congregations that have divided into two groups—the actively involved members and the inactive. This is an exceptionally effective method of perpetuating the we-they division.

A fourth historic response to diversity and pluralism has been to seek to accommodate the divergent religious views which can typically be identified within the one organized religious group. The outstanding example of this has been the Roman Catholic Church. Through the establishment of a variety of orders and other structural innovations, the official recognition of several different rites and other means, the Roman Catholic Church has been able to have unity with diversity. A somewhat similar pattern of accommodating diversity through structures can be seen in several American denominational families. These include the jurisdiction and annual conferences in what is now The United Methodist Church, the former English District in The Lutheran Church—Missouri Synod, the Conferences in the Mennonite Church, the dioceses of the Episcopal Church, and the synods in the old United Lutheran Church in America.

In congregational life the use of this structural approach to accommodate diversity can be seen most clearly in the variety of adult Sunday school classes. This response also is illustrated by the organizing of new circles within the women's organization or by developing a separate program for men's work or by offering two *different* worship experiences on Sunday morning or by developing a multiple-staff ministry and in replacing the one youth fellowship for high school youth with two or three youth groups.

This structural accommodation to pluralism means we have our organizational home, and they have their place within the larger structure.

A fifth response to pluralism which overlaps the second can be seen in those congregations which have *intentionally* developed a pluralistic character.

As was pointed out earlier, research from the Church Growth Movement suggests that a congregation which reaches and serves a very narrow slice of the total population spectrum is more likely to grow than one which happens to be far more heterogeneous in the composition of its membership and in its evangelistic appeal. In simple language, the data suggest that the homogeneous congregation which seeks to reach people of similar characteristics is more likely to be a growing congregation than the diverse congregation which seeks "to minister to everyone" or the relatively homogeneous congregation which seeks to reach people from a different slice of the total spectrum of the population or to reach people from a different subculture.

The response to this from some congregations with a comparatively diverse membership has been to *intentionally* develop a pluralistic style of ministry and a varied and diverse program. The purpose of this is to cause both them and us to feel welcome, wanted, and a sense of belonging and acceptance. Perhaps the simplest illustration of this concept is the congregation which schedules two different services on Sunday, not because of the pressures of space, but as the result of a conscious and intentional effort to offer people a choice between two different worship experiences. Another common example of this approach is the congregation which is contemplating offering on Sunday morning the three choices of (a) worship followed by Sunday school, (b) Sunday school followed by worship, and (c) Sunday school at the same time with worship. This approach is often opposed by the antipluralist who asks, "Why should we have three worship services when the building is large enough to hold all three groups at the same hour? All we're doing is dividing our congregation." The pluralist responds, "We're doing this in response to the fact that our congregation is already divided—some attend only worship, some attend only Sunday school, and many stay away from both."

There is no question that it is very difficult for a congregation to be both a pluralistic parish *and* a rapidly growing church *unless* there is a great emphasis on intentionally offering and *legitimatizing* a comparatively wide range of choices for people. One cost for this is that it usually requires more staff leadership positions than a more homogeneous congregation of the same size. Another price tag is that the intentionally pluralistic congregation usually requires a greater degree of tolerance on the part of the members.

A sixth, and perhaps the most creative, response to the pressures of pluralism can be found in the leadership style of both the ministerial and lay leaders of the congregation or denomination. This style can be summarized in these words: Affirm and build. In broad general terms, it is very unlike the more common response: Criticize and divide.

The creative response is based on three important assumptions. First, it assumes a basic distinction between affirmation and approval. Frequently it is possible to affirm an action, a decision, or a person when it would not be possible to offer unconditional approval. A simple example is the affirmation of the process which produced a particular decision without necessarily approving the nature or content of that decision. Second, this approach assumes that affirmation will be offered only when it can be done authentically. For example, many Christians who do not identify themselves as charismatic, as that word is now frequently used, can authentically affirm the concept of the gifts of the Holy Spirit. Third, this approach assumes that affirmation is a far better foundation on which to build than is negative criticism.

Leaders of this style try always to affirm and to build creatively on that affirmation before offering any negative comments. We try to authentically affirm what they are doing, and they try to affirm what we are doing.

If the intention is to avoid the divisive pressures of pluralism, a seventh response deserves consideration. This requires minimizing the occasions when questions are raised in either-or language and optimizing the occasions when questions are stated in both-and terms. Which translation of the Bible will be used here? Will the youth ministry be developed around a weekly Sunday program or a series of events and experiences which take the youth out of this community? Will the confirmation classes be conducted by the pastor or the laity? Should we renovate the organ or have a special fund drive to help relieve world hunger? Should the Sunday school emphasize learning content or experiential learning techniques? Should we have the youth choir or the adult choir offer special music as part of the worship service?

Each one of these and scores of other questions can be stated in either-or terms or in both-and language. The congregation which seeks to live creatively with pluralism will optimize the both-and style of stating potentially divisive questions while the anti-pluralists will contend that every question must be phrased in either-or language. The use of either-or terminology tends to accentuate the we-they divisions.

Most congregations seeking to function effectively as pluralistic congregations and to minimize the we-they divisions may have to look at a major barrier to a pluralistic congregational life-style. This eighth response to pluralism involves a revision of the traditional system of church governance and decision-making.

The system of church government used in most congregations and in many denominational organizations usually offers people three choices in voting—yes, no, and abstain. Most of these systems of governance are copied from a governmental model rather than being developed from the principles of decision-making in a voluntary organization. By the nature of the organizational structure, the decision-making processes tend to pit us against them.

One result is to focus on counting the no votes, thus encouraging one group of people to tell others what they cannot do. A much more creative, and far less divisive, approach in the increasingly pluralistic congregation is to focus on the yes votes. This approach emphasizes telling people what they can do. Should there be a special Bible study group for eight consecutive Tuesday evenings which will study the Gospel according to Saint Luke? If twelve who vote, "Yes, I would like to do that"; these are more important than the 346 who vote, "No, I am too busy (or tired or occupied with other concerns or watching television) on Tuesday nights to do that."[1]

On most program questions—special fund appeals, modest capital improvements, new ideas for new ministries, and special lay/leadership developing events—the intentionally pluralistic congregation will focus on counting the yes votes rather than the no votes. The anti-pluralist often will insist that all no votes must be counted.

Obviously on major matters of congregation-wide concern, it is often necessary to ask for and count the no votes, but these are comparatively few in number. Changing the system of voting is one method of reducing the tension between us and them.

The ninth in this series of responses to the we-they division, which so often inhibits a congregation's evangelis-

---

[1]For a more detailed explanation of this concept of counting only the yes votes and for guidelines for inaugurating it in a congregation see Lyle E. Schaller and Charles A. Tidwell, *Creative Church Administration* (Nashville: Abingdon, 1975), pp. 38-44.

tic outreach, is rarely undertaken intentionally and knowingly, but is one of the most appropriate responses. A remarkably effective means of minimizing the we-they division in a church and reducing the tensions in a pluralistic congregation is to call a person who was reared as an only child to be the pastor. In approximately seven out of ten cases, the male who was reared as an only child grows up with a high degree of self-esteem, self-confidence, optimism, and cheerfulness. The adult who was reared as an only child has had a lifetime of practice in getting along with two very different adults and subconsciously works hard at relating effectively to people unlike himself. The adult male who was reared as an only child often tends to be a perfectionist, to have a high level of competence in verbal skills, and not to be jealous of others. The male minister who was reared as an only child rarely feels his role as pastor and professional leader of the congregation is threatened by the we-they division and thus is able to authentically affirm both factions.

This we-they division has been given considerable attention here partly because it is a growing phenomenon, partly because it often produces more frustrations than result from any of the other conditions described in this chapter, partly because it often is the major inhibiting factor in a congregation's evangelistic outreach, partly because it is a major barrier to the assimilation of new members, and partly because constructive responses to it have received comparatively little attention.

There is every indication this new pluralism will continue to grow as a factor in the evangelistic outreach and the assimilation of new members by congregations. American society is becoming increasingly varied and diverse. This can be seen in the variety of dress, of life-styles, of vocations, and of housing. This new pluralism can be seen in the move back toward a multilingual society. The growth of pluralism can also be seen in another fundamental change. For generations the dominant pattern was to train people to fit into the existing structures, institutions, organizations, traditions, schedules, and customs of society. For the past three decades this theme has gradually been reversed to change the existing structures, institutions, organizations, traditions, schedules, and customs of society to accommodate people.

This change towards an increasingly pluralistic society also can be seen in the churches as many of what were language or nationality or social class congregations become Americanized and the members are drawn from an ever broader cross section of the American population. Each new generation of adult members tends to increase the diverse nature of the membership. The younger members do not always seek to perpetuate the expectations, values, and customs of the older members. If admitted and permitted to do so, new members tend to bring in new ideas and new ways of carrying out the ministry of the churches. Among the many examples of this are the ex-rural church, the ex-nationality church, old First Church downtown, and many suburban churches established after World War II. The various responses to pluralism described here offer congregations a variety of alternatives as they seek to respond constructively to this us-them syndrome.

Planning for Growth

The tenth and last in this series of circles identifying the dynamics of inclusion and exclusion describes the healthy, growing, and vital congregation that has been increasing its capability to assimilate new members. Ideally this occurs concurrently with the efforts to expand the evangelistic outreach to people outside any worshiping congregation.

In this congregation there are too many fellowship circles to count. The vast majority of the members are actively involved in at least one meaningful group, and many are members of two or three groups. There are three other distinctive characteristics of the congregations represented by diagram 10. First, many of the circles are open, indicating that new members can be accepted. Second, several of the 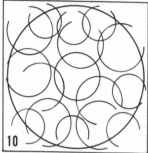 groups include people who are not confirmed members of that parish. This is one of the reasons why this is a growing congregation. Third, there also is room in the membership circle for people who are not members of any fellowship circle or who do not covet that relationship.

Some of these smaller fellowship circles or groups can trace their origins back many years, while others were formed very recently. A distinctive characteristic of this healthy parish is that the members of one group affirm the purpose, existence, and role of other groups.

This pattern is easier to describe than it is to deveop in many congregations. In order to accommodate everyone who might be interested in being a member of a meaningful, small face-to-face group, and also to offer a variety of choices to people, it usually is necessary to have six or seven of these groups or circles for each one hundred members who are thirteen or fourteen years of age or older. This is comparatively easy to accomplish in most one-hundred-member congregations. These groups might include the youth fellowship that meets on Sunday evening, an adult Sunday school class, the women's organization, an evening Bible study group, a choir, the governing board, the Christian education committee, a men's breakfast and prayer group, the trustees, a high school Sunday school class, a building committee, the pastoral relations committee that meets as a support group for the minister, or the group that comes over on the first Saturday of every month to clean the church.

What is far more difficult is to maintain sixty to seventy small face-to-face groups in the thousand-member congregation. It is far easier for all the leaders to function with one-third to one-half that many groups and allow a substantial number of members to drop into a comparatively inactive role. In general, the weaker the glue described in chapter 1, the greater the need for this ratio of face-to-face groups to membership. In general, the larger the proportion of new members who come from a background not identical with the background of the members, the greater the need for this ratio of small groups. In general, the longer the congregation has been functioning from this same location, the greater the need for this ratio of six or seven small face-to-face groups per one hundred members. In general, the more urbanized the community in which the members live, the greater the need for this ratio. In general, the more pluralistic and diverse the membership of the church, the larger the number of program staff members necessary to maintain this ratio.

The thirty-year-old, very homogeneous, thousand-member congregation which still has a strong nationality flavor, which has a beloved pastor in his nineteenth year in this parish, and which also benefits from several of the organizing principles described in chapter 1, may function with a very high participation rate and no other paid program staff members except the pastor. By contrast, the ninety-year-old, very heterogeneous congregation which has no distinctive ethnic, language, or nationality heritage; which saw a twenty-five year pastorate come to an end two or three years ago; and which has only a limited amount of glue holding it together may require two or three full-time program staff positions—*in addition* to the relatively new senior minister—to develop and maintain a ratio of six or seven groups per one hundred members. If it fails to develop these groups it probably either (a) will not grow and/or (b) will not be able to assimilate all of the new members who do unite with that large congregation. At least one-half of the time of one of the staff members should be devoted to the identification, recruitment, training, placement, and continuing support of additional leaders or there will be an unending stream of complaints such as: We can't even find the lay volunteers to lead new groups—It's the same old loyal core carrying the load year after year. Why can't these new people help carry part of the load?

It also probably will be necessary in that type of situation for the time of one full-time staff person, or the equivalent, to be spent in identifying unmet needs, developing new groups in response to these needs, finding leadership for these new groups, and nurturing these new groups. The usual alternative in the large, heterogeneous, and pluralistic congregation is to allow many new members to drop into a comparatively inactive role.

This series of ten circles can be used by congregations of all sizes and types in analyzing the inclusionary and exclusionary characteristics of that church.

Questions for Self-Examination

1. Identify the various groups, classes, circles, choirs, committees, boards, and organizations which together constitute the fellowship circle of your congregation. Include only those where membership and participation in that group is a meaningful relationship with other persons for a majority of the members. If it is strictly a functional group without any significant relational dimensions, do not include it.

2. How many groups are there on the list? What is the ratio per one hundred members?

3. Identify the common characteristics (age, tenure in this congregation, marital status, sex, education, race, nationality, etc.) of the members who are in the largest number of groups. Is there any common pattern?

4. Go over the membership roll name by name, and do the same for the members who are not in any group. Does a common pattern emerge?

5. List the name of each adult who has united with this congregation during the past two years and try to identify the

primary reason why that individual united with this congregation. This can be done most effectively by a separate interview with each recent new member. Compare your results with the discussion accompanying diagram 5 in this chapter.

6. List the names of each adult who has united with this congregation during the past two years. (List a husband and wife couple on separate lines as two individuals.) Opposite each name list (a) the groups in the congregation to which that person belongs *and is an active and participating member,* (b) the roles or offices held by that new member, and (c) the tasks or jobs held by that new member. How well assimilated are the new members who have complete blanks after their names? Who in your congregation is responsible for the assimilation of these new members? Who will follow up on the persons on this list who have no group role or task listed opposite their names?

7. As you look at the program staff of your congregation, both the lay volunteers and the paid staff, including the minister and perhaps a church secretary, ask these questions:

(a) Is your congregation staffed to grow, to remain on a plateau, or to decline in size?

(b) What is the name of the paid staff person who has the responsibility for helping new members, on a one-to-one basis, find a meaningful place in a group; helping organize new small face-to-face groups; or helping that new member find a meaningful role or task? If this is not being done by a paid staff person, is there a lay volunteer who does this?

(c) Who is responsible for lay leadership development in your congregation? Is there a special emphasis on helping new members move into leadership roles?

V
Strengthening the Group Life

"We've tried on three different occasions to start a new adult Sunday school class for young married couples, and each time it falters after a few months; and within a year or so, it's dead," commented a member from Bethel Church.

"We're having a similar problem with the women's auxiliary, the men's group in the church, and other organizations that had been so vital for years."

These are very important questions for the congregation seeking to build a caring and supportive fellowship for people. These also are very important questions for the church concerned with the assimilation of new adult members. For many decades the adult Sunday school classes, the women's organizations, and the men's groups were the most effective means in many congregations for reaching people who were outside any church. These groups and organizations were often a very effective means of reaching newcomers to the community. Thousands of church members were assimilated into the life of what initially was to them a congregation of strangers through one of these face-to-face, small groups.

In addition to providing a very meaningful supportive fellowship for individuals and supplying a comfortable point of entry for the assimilation of new members, these organizations usually offer a variety of very significant opportunities for the personal and spiritual growth of the members. In thousands of churches the opportunities provided by these small groups for the personal and spiritual growth of the members are very meaningful to huge numbers of individuals. With some members these experiences are more significant than corporate worship.

In some respects it could be argued that the strength of these small face-to-face groups has led to the decline of the adult Sunday school in many denominations, to the fading away of the men's groups, and to the deterioration of the women's organizations in hundreds and hundreds of congregations. That condition is a perceived rivalry between the small face-to-face groups and the church. Frequently, this is described by statements such as "They're a church within the church" or "That class is really a small clique that runs this church" or "Decisions here are made at board meetings, but the question of which of those decisions will be implemented is answered at the monthly meeting of the men's club."

These comments carry the discussion back to the various responses to pluralism described in the preceding chapter. One of the most important factors in helping a congregation respond effectively to the challenge of pluralism is the quality of the group life. This also may be the most important single factor in that church's ability to assimilate new members.

Unfortunately, however, many church leaders tend to focus on the negative values of closely knit, cohesive groups rather than seeing them as foundation stones for the evangelistic outreach of that congregation and in the assimilation of new members. Too often these small groups are seen as cliques, rivals, power blocs, and closed clubs. The ironic part of this is that the more meaningful membership in that small face-to-face group is to the persons in it, the more threatening it often appears to be to the individuals not in it. This frequently includes the pastor, denominational program staff and specialists, and other church leaders with a predominantly functional, rather than a relational, view of the church.

How to Kill a New Sunday School Class for Young Couples

In addition to this widespread and slightly paranoid fear of strong and meaningful small face-to-face groups, many congregations have developed a very high level of competence in killing off emerging new groups. This can be illustrated by looking at the unintentional procedures that have been developed to stifle the emergence of a new Sunday school class for young married couples. By reflecting on these sixteen points it may be possible to avoid some of the frustrations that have been produced in so many congregations where a serious effort to organize such a new class was undercut by a series of unrelated and well-intentioned, but counterproductive, actions.

1. Ask two or three of the wives who are very interested in organizing this new class to teach a Sunday school class in the children's department.

2. Ask one or two of the husbands who are heavily involved in this class to accept other responsibilities that will divert their time and energy from the class.

3. Limit the number of social get-togethers to a maximum of four per year in order to prevent the development of strong relational ties among members of the class.

4. Discourage any class project since projects tend to help strengthen the feeling of cohesiveness among members of any organization.

5. Encourage some new younger couples to join older classes in order to bring young blood into these classes.

6. Every four to six months ask the class to move to a different room since attachment to a familiar place can strengthen the members' ties to that group.

7. If the creation of this class reflects a high priority in outreach and an emphasis by this congregation to strengthen its outreach to adults born after World War II, hide the meeting place for this class in some obscure and hard-to-find

room in the building. Encourage the following three classes to occupy the three classrooms that have the highest visibility to a stranger, are the easiest to find, and are closest to the main entrance to the building: (1) a class for elderly ladies, (2) a class for married couples born in the 1920-35 era, and (3) a class for persons born before 1920.

8. Schedule very important meetings for young parents during the Sunday school hour.

9. Discourage this class from identifying itself with a distinctive name. Adoption of a name helps people identify themselves as members of that group or organization. Keep the emphasis on a holistic approach to Christian education and on membership in the congregation, rather than encouraging young couples to identify with this class.

10. Actively discourage the creation of a distinctive name tag to be worn by members. First of all, these symbols create a sense of class unity. Second, name tags help people remember the names of others, and this tends to strengthen the sense of belonging to that group.

11. Instead of using a "both-and" approach be sure to identify the emerging new class as a potential rival of the Sunday morning worship experience. The best method for developing divided loyalties and encouraging a sense of rivalry is to schedule this class for the same hour as the corporate worship experience or to conflict with one of the worship services in the church that offers two worship experiences on Sunday morning.

12. As soon as the class reaches a comfortable size and begins to develop its own identity as a group, divide the class. This can be accomplished by any one of several methods such as dividing the class to form two new classes, by the forced graduation from the class when members reach a certain age, by requiring all adult classes to take a six- or eight-week recess to enable the members to participate in special elective courses, or by reshuffling the membership of all adult classes every year or two.

13. Discourage the class from meeting during the sum-

mer. A disproportionately large number of young couples change their place of residence during the summer. By not meeting during the summer months this class can decrease the number of new young members who might find this class to be a good entry point into that congregation. By fall the backlog of young couples who moved into the community may be large enough that this class will not be able to assimilate more than two or three of the young couples who have come into this congregation during the previous three or four months. Most classes of this type find it difficult to adequately assimilate more than one new couple every six to eight weeks. Thus some of the September visitors from the summer backlog probably will be discouraged from coming back Sunday after Sunday.

14. Keep the emphasis in the class on education and on learning content. Discourage anything, such as a coffee, rolls, conversation period for fifteen minutes before the class begins, or parties, outings, and social events that would reinforce the interpersonal relationships and the friendship ties among the members.

15. Vigorously encourage the concept of a unified budget for the entire congregation and discourage individual classes from having their own treasuries. A person's heart follows, as well as leads, his or her treasure. When members make financial contributions to their own class treasury, it reinforces a sense of loyalty to that class.

16. Prohibit the selection of a gifted, attractive, and skilled permanent teacher during that first year. Bringing a collection of individuals together under the leadership of a talented permanent teacher has proved to be one of the most effective means of developing a cohesive group.

This list should be taken very seriously. Every item on it has been tested by the experience of many different congregations. Any congregation willing to follow even eight or ten of these procedures can almost guarantee that it will be impossible for anyone to successfully launch a new Sunday school class for young married couples. On the other hand, if your congregation is interested in organizing new adult classes it might be informative to discover how many of these tested procedures are being observed unknowingly or unintentionally.

Is There a Future for the Men's Fellowship?

Perhaps the most widespread source of frustration in nurturing and strengthening the group life of the typical congregation is the difficulty encountered by those who are seeking to build a strong men's group. This appears to be the program area filled with the largest number of struggling groups, corpses, recollections of formerly strong organizations, frustrated dreams, and unfulfilled visions. In looking at those congregations where there are healthy and vital organizations for men, several characteristics stand out repeatedly. While there is no guarantee that observance of all these criteria will produce a strong men's group, they are worthy of consideration. There are enough congregations with vigorous men's fellowships to suggest they still meet a significant need in many churches.

First, most of the strongest men's groups have a central purpose of mission and/or service. The vital groups rarely are built solely around entertainment, fellowship, or nostalgia.

Second, the healthiest organizations for men usually include one or two men who are effective leaders, work hard at this job, take it very seriously, and are convinced of the value of a separate men's organization.

Third, the pastor believes in the concept, is very supportive, and usually attends every meeting of the group. This is as important for the female pastor as it is for the male minister. One of the most effective means of killing off a men's organization is for the minister to be opposed to it.

Fourth, the group usually has at least one annual project which requires people to work with their hands. This may be constructing a new sidewalk around the church property, painting one or two Sunday school rooms every year, rehabilitating a house for a low income or a refugee family, holding an annual barbecue to raise money for missions, putting a new roof on the church building, remodeling the parsonage, pursuing a Lord's Acre project in a farming community, or having a quarterly meeting to clean the church building.

The annual project always requires more hands; therefore, it is an easy entrance point for newcomers, for shy and less articulate persons, and for persons with special skills. It is a community-building experience (see item 11 in chapter 1). It provides a sense of satisfaction and accomplishment for the men when it is completed. It offers a chance for husbands to brag to their wives. It requires the use of creative skills. It can be carried out during spare hours.

Fifth, in one form or another there is a strong emphasis on meeting the spiritual needs of the men. The most common example of this is the men's Bible study and prayer group that meets at an early hour one morning every week.

Sixth, there is one social event annually to which wives and sweethearts are invited.

Seventh, the value and legitimacy of the group is recognized by its being listed as one of the official organizations of the church.

Eighth, on a regional or a state level there is an annual inspirational event for men sponsored by the denomination. The central thrust of this event is the spiritual growth of the participants. It is *not* a promotional or educational or recreational or church-business event.

Ninth, there is at least one person in the regional judicatory of the denomination who has the portfolio for men's work and who personally is a proponent of strong and vital men's fellowships.

Tenth, if the men's group is in recreation or sports, it is more likely to do this as an outreach project for others (children, couples, neighborhood youth, etc.) than for the members themselves.

Eleventh, the vital men's group almost invariably has its

own treasury and thus is able to respond to specific needs directly and unilaterally without giving through the official machinery of the church.

Finally, but not last in importance, the men's group eats together at least eight times a year. One of the most effective means of killing the men's organization in a church is to eliminate the opportunity for the men to eat together.

There are enough vital men's organizations in the churches today to counter the widely heard observation that such groups belong to the past. Most of the healthiest groups display eight to ten of the characteristics identified here. That may not be a coincidence.

What's Ahead for the Women's Organization?

In many congregations the women's organization has been the most effective of all the educational operations. Frequently, it also has been the most missions-oriented organization, the most progressive social-action element, the group most sensitive to the needs of neighbors, and the most meaningful channel for the personal and spiritual growth of individuals in the entire congregation. Yet, despite this very impressive record from the past, the women's organization in many congregations is beginning to wither away. Why? Perhaps in examining two responses to that Why? some clues can be found that will be helpful in creative planning for today and tomorrow.

In several denominations the original focus of the women's organization was the support and expansion of the missionary work of that denomination. Frequently, the word "missionary" was a part of the official name of the organization. As a result, for years, or perhaps even decades, the women's organization in each congregation had a clearly defined, highly visible, specific, usually measurable (How much money did we raise for missions this past year?), and unifying central purpose. In support of this purpose of furthering the missionary outreach of the denomination, the

106

members of the local women's organization in each congregation spent considerable time and energy in Bible study, prayer, the study of missionary work, money-raising endeavors, meeting and talking with missionaries on furlough, and in fellowship with one another. These activities, however, were not the basic reason for the existence of the group, but rather were supportive of, and fringe benefits of, the central purpose. For decades in several denominations the women's missionary auxiliary was either the only, or the major, supporter of the foreign missionary work of that denomination. These women knew that what they were doing was more than important; it was absolutely essential to the continuation of the missionary work of that denomination.

Eventually, however, in many denominational families this basic responsibility for foreign missions was shifted from the women's organization to a denomination-wide organizational structure which turned to the congregation, rather than to the local women's auxiliaries for the basic financial support of missions.

The result was (1) the elimination or the reduction in importance of the distinctive purpose of the women's auxiliary in each congregation (what had once been "our" responsibility was now a shared responsibility) (2) the elimination of the very *unifying* sense of purpose that had been a part of each local auxiliary for so long, and (3) the elimination of that meaningful task (the support of missionaries) which not only had been the glue that held each auxiliary together but which also kept the door wide open for newcomers to come into that auxiliary. The old saying, "When you know you are needed, you know you belong" gradually became less applicable as the basic purpose of many local women's auxiliaries turned from missions to fellowship.

A second basic reason for the decline of the women's organization in many congregations was identified in the previous chapter. This is the increasingly pluralistic nature of

American society. There are at least three dimensions to this that have relevance here.

First, how should the local auxiliary be organized into circles or sub-groups? Most responses to this question fall into one of three categories. At Church A there are three circles. One meets in the morning, one in the afternoon, and one in the evening. At Church B there are five circles. One is a Bible study circle; a second is responsible for dinners, wedding receptions, etc.; a third circle is composed of women who call on shut-ins; a fourth circle manages the annual bazaar; and a fifth carries out the responsibilities of the altar guild, which was transformed into a circle in the hopes of attracting younger women. At Church C there are six circles. One is made up exclusively of young (under 30) mothers, a second is composed of older retired women and began years ago as a circle for business and professional women, a third consists of women of various ages and marital status who seek to be part of a weekly Bible study and prayer group, a fourth includes those women who are interested in arts and crafts, a fifth is for mothers of young (pre-first grade) children, and a sixth is for women who have a strong interest in various forms of community ministries.

In summary, at Church A the circles are organized around when they meet, at Church B the common organizing principle is what that circle does, and at Church C that structure is oriented toward the persons who constitute each circle. Which is the best organizational principle to follow? The right answer in a pluralistic congregation is "yes, all three." The basic organizing principle should affirm all three approaches. The use of only one, and particularly of either of the first two, will tend to reduce the number of choices and narrow the degree of participation.

Second, there has been a growing wave of sentiment that the role of women in the church should not be limited to any one organization, but rather that they should have complete equality with men and be eligible to hold any office in the church. This is a commendable goal, and in recent years significant progress has been made in achieving it in many congregations. Unfortunately, however, this often has been presented in either-or terms rather than in both-and terms, with the implication that the existence of a women's auxiliary represents a major barrier to full equality for women. This is an elitist approach. An affirmation of pluralism approach would begin by eliminating that very common sexist, but usually irrelevant, statement that "every woman member of this congregation is a member of the women's organization" and affirming the rights of women to hold any leadership position in the congregation, and also affirming the rights of women to form and manage their own organization. In an intentionally pluralistic church some women will prefer to devote their time and talents to congregational leadership responsibilities, some will prefer to work within and through the women's organization, some will do both, and others will not be interested in either. The members of this last group will not be made to feel guilty about their choice.

Third, there is a recent increase in the proportion of women employed outside the home. In 1947, there were 29.9 million husbands and 6.5 million wives in the labor force. By 1977, the number of working husbands had gone up 31 percent to 39 million, but the number of working wives had increased 224 percent to 21 million. In 1948, one-fourth of the mothers with children age 6-17 were employed outside the home. By 1977, that proportion had doubled to 51.2 percent. In 1977, only 7 percent of all families in the United States were composed of a husband and a wife, living together with children under eighteen at home and the wife not in the labor force. Ninety-three percent of all families did not meet all three of those criteria, yet in many congregations the program and schedule is developed on the premise that the typical family does meet them.

The women's organizations in the churches were founded in the era when relatively few women had an income of their own. Meeting times, program-planning, money-raising projects, and opportunities for personal and spiritual growth

109

were developed to reflect that era. Today's women's organization needs to be able to be responsive to the needs, schedules, and resources of women who are not employed outside the home, to those who have jobs, and to those who go in and out of the labor force at irregular intervals.

The future of the women's organization in the churches may be determined by their success in redefining a unifying definition of purpose, by their response to pluralism, by their ability to resist the normal pressures to become exclusionary, by their capacity to set new goals that are meaningful to a new generation of women, by their refusal to become an issue-oriented organization (which almost invariably is very divisive), by their emphasis on the relational rather than the functional dimensions of life, and by their resistance of the institutional temptations that have killed many organizations in the churches.

Other Alternatives

The emphasis here on these three organizations is not intended to suggest they are the only channels for strengthening the group life of the congregation or for opening new doors for the assimilation of new members. Each one is important; and in many congregations the Sunday school, the women's organization, and the men's fellowship, together with the youth program,[1] constitute the heart of the group life in that parish.

There are several additional alternatives, however, for reinforcing and expanding the group life of a congregation. Among these are prayer circles; the Bethel Bible classes; Yokefellow groups with their discipline of Bible study, prayer, and outreach; the pastor's class for new members; therapy groups; choirs; drama groups; marriage enrichment

---

[1]For suggestions on strengthening the youth program see Schaller, *Survival Tactics in the Parish,* pp. 144-54.

classes and retreats; quilting circles; the Fishermen's Club, which carries out a ministry of visitation evangelism; athletic teams; groups built around the expression of creative gifts in crafts and in the arts; Bible study groups that meet during the evening; and groups for special categories of individuals such as the recently widowed, the families who have experienced the death of a child, single parents, single young adults, mature adults, and travel groups. Many of the principles, cautions, and considerations identified earlier as factors in the Sunday school class, the men's fellowship, and the women's organization will apply to other types of groups.

Four Caution Signs

In planning for the reinforcement of the group life of a congregation there are four caution signs that merit special emphasis here.

First, if at all possible, avoid a forced division of any existing class, group, choir, or circle. Create a new group. Some members of an existing group may decide to become a part of this new group. New groups tend to be more open to new people than do the groups which are a product of dividing long-established groups. In general, change by addition is more creative and less traumatic than change by division or subtraction.

Second, an annual review of the group life of the congregation should be conducted to evaluate the balance. This is both a balance in terms of groups for all segments of the congregation and a balance between the personal and spiritual growth of the individual and the outreach of the congregation to people and needs beyond the membership.

Third, recognize *and affirm* the fact that some groups become closed fellowship circles, and it becomes very difficult for these groups to receive and accept new members. Instead of harassing the members in these groups who value this supportive fellowship, start new groups.

Fourth, view with great skepticism any proposal for creating new groups on a functional or geographical basis or in response to the institutional needs of the church.

The most widespread example of this is the "zone plan" or "undershepherd program" or "parish group" which divides the member households on the basis of lines drawn on a map. The program usually is designed to facilitate the care of the members and improve communication between the church and the members. While some churches have been successful in making this plan work and it has produced the desired results, a far larger proportion have encountered major frustrations and disappointments. In general, the larger the congregation, the greater the difficulty and the larger the amount of staff time required to maintain the network. In general, the longer the system is in operation, the greater the burden of maintaining the zone-plan network. In general, the greater the compatibility of the structure of the zone plan with the total life of the congregation, the fewer the difficulties in maintaining the system.

In reviewing the experiences of scores of congregations which have established zone plans or parish groups or undershepherd plans or some other variation on this basic idea, several points repeatedly appear.

1. Some members do not want to be a part of any group.

2. In many congregations perhaps one-fifth to one-half or more of the resident members already are actively in a group which can, and often does, provide the oversight and care desired. Do not disturb these by asking the members to be in some other group.

3. People tend not to live in geographic neighborhoods. Rather, their social interchange and interpersonal relationships usually are on a nongeographic basis. (In other words, use a "map" of interpersonal relationships, not a street map, in establishing new groups.)

4. Select the leaders. Do not broadcast an appeal for volunteers.

5. Train all group leaders.

6. The ideal size of a group is between eight and seventeen persons.

7. It is unrealistic to assume that because a member expresses a willingness to serve on the board, that member has a gift for calling and the pastoral care of people. In the denominational families where each member of the governing board oversees one zone or group, the elders or deacons are chosen primarily for these gifts in pastoral care. It may take four or five years to institutionalize this concept.

8. Some people have a gift for visitation-evangelism calling but not for pastoral oversight, and some people have a gift for calling on members and friends but not on strangers. Serving as a leader in this program and serving as a caller requires two different sets of gifts.

9. In any training program there usually tends to be a 60 to 80 percent drop-off in effectiveness when the individual who is trained for a responsibility goes out to train someone else in that responsibility.

In summary, the zone plan or undershepherd program is really a highly functional concept, and most people live, think, function, and act in terms of relationships. That is not only a basic caution in establishing a zone plan, but it also is a very useful principle for any effort to strengthen the group life of a congregation.

Questions for Self-Examination

1. Do you have a class for young married couples? If you do, ask the members (or the leaders) of that class to take the checklist in the first part of this chapter and discover what has happened, or not happened, to that class. How many of these sixteen points apply? If you no longer have a class for young married couples, did it die or fade away? Were any of these sixteen items important factors in its demise? If they were, who has the responsibility to do something about it?

2. Do you have a men's fellowship group? If you do, ask

the leaders to review the checklist for that organization. If you do not have such a group, are these some of the reasons for its absence?

3. Ask the leaders of the women's organization to read the section directed to that group.

4. How many new circles or subgroups are planned for this coming year? Describe the specific characteristics of the people this new circle will seek to reach.

5. What proportion of the women in your congregation are employed outside the home? What proportion of circles or subgroups in the women's organization are intended for women employed outside the home? How do these two percentages compare?

6. In your congregation who has the basic responsibility for evaluating the group life of the congregation and for suggesting the creation of new groups?

VI
Looking at the Inactive Members

"How do you activate the inactive members?" asked George Bennett a member of the group in general and the resource person in particular. George was one of three dozen lay leaders from fourteen congregations who were attending a weekend workshop on evangelism and church growth. "I don't want to minimize the importance of reaching the unchurched with the gospel, and I agree that it is important that a Christian should be a part of the nurturing fellowship of a church," he continued, "but we have a bigger problem. Before coming here this weekend I did some homework. During the past four years we have received thirty-nine new adult members. I'm counting only adults, not the children of members who grew up in the church or the youth who joined with their parents. Out of this list of thirty-nine adults who joined during the past four years, nine have moved out of our community, seven are very active members, twelve are moderately active, and eleven are either completely, or almost totally, inactive. Now, can you give me some help on that one? More than a third of those who still live in our community are inactive."

"That's a better record than we have at First Church," commented Glenn Frazier. "I don't have the exact figures, but my guess is that at least half of the new adult members we receive become inactive within five years after they join our congregation."

"That's high on our priority list, too," added Martha Thomas from Bethany Church. "How can we strengthen the commitment of our members so we don't end up with so

115

many inactive members? And I'm also interested in what we can do about all who are now inactive."

"I guess it's the same all over," offered a second representative from the fourteen-hundred-member First Church. "Many of the church organizations which used to have so much vitality and which meant so much to so many people simply aren't attracting people today. We have a lot of members on the roll who are almost completely inactive. I guess everyone is so busy these days they don't seem to have time for church activities anymore."

"We've tried a half dozen different procedures," responded an older man from Trinity Church. "Once a year we call on all our inactive members and urge them to begin attending church again, but it doesn't seem to help. Two years ago we visited every inactive member during November and urged them to attend during Advent. In February of last year we went out again and called on every inactive member and invited them to attend every Sunday during Lent, but it didn't do much good. Only a handful responded."

"Let's face it," declared a member from the Lake Avenue Church. "We're talking about people who don't care. They simply want their names on the membership roll of some church, but they're not interested in being a part of it or in supporting it. All they want is their names on the membership roster."

"Let's get down to the key issue," insisted a determined member of the Main Street Church. "What's wrong with these people who come forward and unite with the church in apparent sincerity and then drop out? Why do these people behave that way? What is there about people that causes them to want to join a church, but not be willing to take any responsibility? Why is it some people insist on being members of a church, but they won't participate in any program or activity or group in that church?"

The best response to these comments is that they are very, very poor questions. They are poor because the wording transfers the responsibility for the present state of affairs from us to them. That is a loser.

All we have direct control over is what we do or do not do. We do not have direct control over what they do or do not do. Therefore a better question to ask is, What did we do or not do that may have helped create this set of conditions? While this may be a very threatening question to raise, it can be a far more constructive approach than speculating about what is wrong with them. This can be illustrated by reviewing some of the most widely shared assumptions on this subject.

Assumptions About Inactive Members

The easiest approach to the question of inactive members, why they are inactive, and what can be done about it, is to focus on the faults of the inactive members. Why did they not take their vows of membership more seriously? Why do some people seem to be more concerned that their names are on the membership roll than about the obligations of church membership? Why do those people expect the rest of us to be willing to support this congregation so it can be here when they decide it is convenient to attend worship?

While this scapegoating approach may be an enjoyable hobby for many people, it tends not to be especially helpful or productive. It is an especially poor approach for the congregation that is seriously interested in the assimilation of recent new members. A better approach might be to look at the issue of inactive members from this set of assumptions.

1. We assume that every person who united with this congregation did so with complete sincerity and in good faith.

2. We assume that every person who united with this congregation and is now an inactive member has what is, from their point of view, a good reason for being inactive.

3. We assume that if each inactive member has a good reason for being inactive they will continue to be inactive until after that reason has been identified and eliminated.

117

(Therefore any effort to make the inactive members feel more guilty about being inactive probably will be counter-productive.)

4. We assume that for us to speculate and attempt to identify that reason will be less productive than seeking to discover that reason more directly by talking with the inactive member.

5. We assume that since all our inactive members are normal human beings they will respond like other normal human beings and offer excuses rather than reasons when we first approach them. (If we accept their excuses as reasons or if we try to dismiss these excuses as unimportant, we may never discover the real reasons behind the excuses.)

6. We assume that we can learn more by listening than by talking, and therefore our approach to our inactive members will be one of active listening.[1] We can expect this to require at least several hours of active listening with each inactive member or inactive family.

7. We assume this listening process is more likely to require six to ten hours, rather than two or three hours, if we are serious about getting beyond the veneer of excuses and discovering the basic reasons why this member is now inactive.

8. We assume this process will probably require several visits, and it is unlikely to be accomplished in one or two visits. (Frequently the first visit produces a series of excuses and guilt responses by the inactive member, the second visit releases a variety of hostile comments, and not until the third or fourth visit is the caller able to hear the basic reasons why this person is now inactive.)

9. We assume that the longer we wait after a member has become inactive, the more difficult it will be to help that person become an active member of this congregation.

---

[1]For an extended discussion of this type of listening call see "Those Blinking Red Lights" in Lyle E. Schaller, *Hey, That's Our Church!* (Nashville: Abingdon, 1975), pp. 116-25.

10. We assume that few, if any of the existing classes, circles, organizations, and face-to-face groups in this congregation are completely effective in caring for the members of that class or group, in listening and responding constructively to their hurts, anxieties and concerns, or in being sensitive to the needs of persons not in that class or group. Therefore we need a backup system to reach and minister to the people who are not cared for by the face-to-face groups, or we will always be faced with the problem of inactive members.

11. We assume that the person who has become an inactive member often has greater difficulty in coping with feelings of helplessness, hopelessness, anger, hostility, anxiety, or neglect than do the more active members of the congregation.[2] Therefore it is of critical importance that (a) the inactive member be called on before these feelings have become deeply ingrained and (b) that the caller be the type of personality and possess the skills which will *not* further intensify and enhance these feelings of inadequacy and guilt, will rather help the inactive member overcome these feelings.

12. We assume that the vast majority of inactive members send a signal to the church when they experience an anxiety-producing conflict or sense of helplessness.[3] If this signal is ignored, the member may enter into a period of inactivity to further test "whether anyone really cares about me." After the end of this test or probationary period that person becomes an increasingly rigid, inactive member. Therefore it is very important that (a) every congregation have some system for identifying the early signals sent to the church by the potentially inactive members and (b) a system

---

[2]Unquestionably the best resource on this subject is John S. Savage, *The Apathetic and Bored Church Member* (Pittsford, N.Y.: Lead Consultants, P. O. Box 311, 1976).
[3]Schaller, *Hey, That's Our Church!*

for quickly responding to these signals, such as a cadre of trained callers who regularly make listening calls.

13. We assume that the spiritual needs of some members change as the years go by. Therefore some of our longtime members who may appear to have become inactive or who are shopping for a new church home should be identified, not as bored or apathetic or hostile or disinterested, but rather as potential graduates from our congregation.[4] These are the persons who have benefited from everything our congregation has been able to offer them, and as graduates are seeking a postgraduate level of challenge in terms of their own personal religious experience and discipline. If our church cannot or does not offer this, they will look elsewhere. (This migration is both from the liberal churches to the conservative churches and from the conservative churches to the liberal churches. One of the reasons this migration baffles many people is that many of the pastors of liberal churches have been part of the conservative-to-liberal migration while today many lay persons are in the liberal-to-conservative migration pattern.) A constructive response is for the congregation to be prepared to offer a new and varied assortment of events and experiences for the personal and spiritual growth of the members.

14. We assume that in establishing meaningful communication with inactive members we are faced with two challenges. One is to listen (see item 6 above). The second is to be aware of the assumptions we bring to the conversation with the inactive member and to recognize which of our assumptions may be counterproductive.

15. Finally, we assume that while we do not have direct control over all the many factors that may cause a member to be inactive, we do have complete and direct control over the assumptions on which we build our response to the inactive

---

[4]For a very provocative elaboration of this concept see John E. Biersdorf, *Hunger for Experience* (New York: The Seabury Press, 1975).

member as well as over what we do or do not do that causes members to become inactive.

Questions for Self-Examination

1. List the actual operational assumptions for the response of your congregation to new members. How does that list compare with the fifteen assumptions suggested here? Which ones may require changing? What are the major obstacles to changing these operational assumptions in your congregation? How will you overcome these obstacles?

2. You may want to ask the members of the committee or group in your congregation who are responsible for the assimilation of new members to spend a few minutes on this exercise.

You have just returned from a group interview with seven adults who have united with Faith Church during the past three months. Faith is a nine-hundred-member, family-oriented congregation founded in 1953, and today over one-half of the members live more than one mile from the church building.

Herbert Stone, age 49, and his wife Helen, age 46, moved here four months ago from another state. During the discussion Herb said, "One reason we picked Faith is that it's a big church. Helen and I have been members of four different churches in the twenty-five years we have been married. They were all in the two- to five-hundred-member category, and we both became very active in each of the last three. Our youngest child graduates from high school next June, and so when we moved here we thought we would look for a big church we could get lost in and let some others carry the load for a while. Helen and I both feel we're due a vacation for a year or two." Herb and Helen rarely miss worship on Sunday morning, but they are not active in any other area of the life of Faith Church.

Betty Lyons is a twenty-six-year-old, single adult who has an excellent job as a legal secretary in the largest law firm in the county. She came here seven months ago because she wanted to live in this part of the country. She commented, "The only thing that disappoints me about Faith Church is there is no drama group. I love to help with amateur plays. I can do anything—direct, work backstage, act, or whatever is needed. I just love the theater." For the first few months at Faith Church, Betty attended the Pairs and Spares Sunday school class, and it was because of the friendship ties she developed through that class that she decided to transfer her church membership to Faith Church, despite the fact that this meant changing denominations. Lately, however, she has begun to realize that this class is primarily for couples and for persons whose spouses are teaching in the Sunday school or are in the choir and who miss Sunday school because of the extended warm-up period for the choir before worship. Now Betty rarely attends Sunday school but is usually in worship.

Jim and Dottie Wingard are a young married couple in their mid-twenties who have found a home in the Pairs and Spares Class. Dottie also is a member of the young mother's circle in the women's organization, and Jim soon will be asked to serve on the Christian Education committee next year with the hope that he will help the youth program. Both have been active in churches since childhood, and while they moved here only five months ago, they are highly enthusiastic about everything at Faith Church.

Mrs. Charles Parker's husband died eleven months ago. She is sixty-eight years old and decided to leave her friends behind and move two hundred miles in order to be near her son and his wife and three children. This son married a very devout Roman Catholic girl seventeen years ago and today is a very active and committed Catholic. This means that every Sunday morning Mrs. Parker comes here by herself from her apartment two miles west of the church. After visiting here for three months, she was formally received by letter as a member of Faith Church. She never misses Sunday morning worship and never participates in any other program at Faith.

Mrs. Melvin Sparks is a twenty-two-year-old bride of thirteen months who is now eight months pregnant. She comes from a very active church family, but married a man with no church affiliation. They moved here from another part of the state eleven months ago. After trying for several months to persuade her husband to join with her, two months ago she gave up and transferred her membership from her home church to Faith. She has missed worship only three Sundays in the past eleven months (her husband came with her twice several months ago), but is not active in any other aspect of the life of Faith Church.

Ask the members of your group, after they have had the chance to read this material, to discuss these five situations.

First, which of these seven recent new adult members of Faith Church are likely to become completely assimilated into this congregation, to feel a strong sense of belonging, and to become active workers and/or leaders at Faith? Which ones are not likely to become more actively involved in the total life and program at Faith Church? Ask each respondent to give specific reasons for their predictions on each person.

Second, what is the only safe assumption one can offer about all seven?

Third, a total of twelve recent adult, new members were invited to this group interview. Those invited included three couples, two single men in their twenties, one widow, two single women, and one woman (Mrs. Sparks) who belonged, but her husband did not attend because he is not a member. One of the couples, the two single men, and one of the two single women did not attend. What is the only safe assumption one can offer about why these five recent adult new members did not attend?

Fourth, were these seven members sending the church a signal by their non-attendance?

VII
The Price of Growth

"We are convinced that Redeemer Church has the potential to double in size during the next seven years," began the first paragraph of the summary sheet of an exhaustive church growth study. This report had been prepared by a special task force of this twenty-six-year-old congregation which averaged 205 in attendance at Sunday morning worship.

The next paragraph of the report included the following declaration:

> Achievement of this goal will require congregational approval of several changes from our present style of ministry, schedules, and system of priorities. While it is not the most important, the most urgent item on this list of changes is approval of a change in our Sunday morning schedule from one to two worship services. This also will require shutting off the balcony and closing the large door to the overflow room, and 150 in the pews in the nave. If we shift to two worship services effective September 1, we expect that by next spring we will be averaging 120 at the first service and 135 at the second service. That is more than a 20 percent increase over our present attendance level. That will mean the sanctuary will be comfortably full at both services, but there will be room for growth. Unless the congregation approves this schedule change, we do not believe it will be possible to achieve the goal of doubling in size in seven years.

At a subsequent congregational meeting the members at Redeemer voted 126 to 31 to adopt the goal of doubling in size in seven years and by a 98 to 62 margin rejected the recommendation to change to two worship services on Sunday morning.

This pair of decisions illustrates the fact that church growth has a price tag on it, and many congregations are not willing to pay the price of growth. These decisions at Redeemer Church also illustrate the item that stands at the top of this list of price tags on church growth. It may be helpful to conclude this discussion by identifying several of them.

1. The most crucial is the attitude of the members. The first part of this consists of the distinction between wanting to grow and deciding to grow. At Redeemer the members voted by a four-to-one margin that they wanted to grow. When it came to a crucial decision to enable church growth to occur, however, they rejected the necessary change in the Sunday morning schedule to enable growth to occur.

A second part of this is the enthusiasm level of the members. A common characteristic of growing congregations is that members are enthusiastic about their faith as Christians; about the congregation of which they are members; and about the life, program, and ministry of that congregation. A high level of enthusiasm is a major price tag in church growth.

Closely related to that is the intensity of belief. The members of growing churches have intense convictions about their faith and about their call to reach the unchurched.

Another critical element in the attitudes of the people is that the members recognize that they do have considerable control over what happens. God has given us the freedom to make choices. One of these choices concerns the members' attitudes toward the people outside any worshiping congregation. Another choice concerns the response of recent new members. Thus the right answer to the question at the end of chapter 6, What will happen with the seven new members of Faith Church? is one of control. The leaders, by what they do and by what they do not do, have a very large degree of control over which of these seven members will become very active in the life and program at Faith Church. A passive attitude by the members is a surrender of responsibility. An active recognition of the control that the members have over what happens is a basic price tag on church growth.

2. The capability of a congregation to receive, welcome, and assimilate new members is the second most important price tag on growth. It is easier to join most churches than it is to be accepted and to be assimilated into the fellowship of that congregation. That is why the assimilation of new members is the basic theme of this book.

3. The size and variety of the group life must expand as a congregation increases in size. This is a price many congregations are unwilling to pay, as can be seen most clearly in the single-cell churches which refuse to pay the price of becoming multi-cell congregations in order to grow.

4. An essential component of the decision by a congregation to grow in numbers is a recognition that an individual's personal decision to accept Christ as Lord and Savior, the act of uniting with a particular congregation, and the acceptance of that new member into that congregation by the other members are three separate, unrelated, and distinct steps.[1] Too often it is assumed they are one and the same. A recognition of this fact of the process of Christian commitment is a seriously neglected price tag on church growth.

5. High on this list of the price tags of growth is the need to define in precise terms who this congregation is seeking to reach, to identify their specific needs, and to determine how this congregation will respond to those needs.

6. Frequently church members assume that church growth means more of the same. They expect that their congregation can double in size without any significant change in the qualitative dimensions of congregational life.

---

[1]For a provocative visual presentation of the concept that distinguishes between the act of accepting Jesus Christ as Lord and Savior and a person's acceptance into the Body of Christ or assimilation into a worshiping congregation, see James F. Engel and W. Wilbert Norton, *What's Gone Wrong with the Harvest?* (Grand Rapids: Zondervan, 1975).

This is an illusion. An acceptance of change is a price of growth.

7. Frequently church growth is dependent on the quality and quantity of the professional staff leaderership. A growing congregation usually must expand its staff to accommodate a growing number of members. The neglect of that factor can be seen most clearly in the congregations that have built a very large building to accommodate a much larger number of people and then meet the mortgage payments from the salaries of staff who are not hired. They end up as an overbuilt, understaffed, and frustrated congregation.

While there is no evidence that long pastorates produce church growth, rarely does a congregation experience long and *sustained* rapid growth without the benefit of a long pastorate. Short pastorates tend to encourage peaks and valleys in the congregation's growth pattern. The continuity of a long pastorate tends to be an overlooked price tag in church growth.

8. A frequently overlooked price tag on church growth is the importance of defining evangelism in terms of people, not geography. The *primary* emphasis in the evangelistic outreach of the growing church is on the needs of people, not on their places of residence.

9. Perhaps the most subtle item on this list is the need to avoid turning the Christian faith into a cultural religion. This is a centuries-old problem and one which Jesus faced repeatedly. Cultural religion becomes exclusionary, concerned with its own self-preservation, and is blind to the real implications of the gospel. Sinful man, however, often tries to turn Christian churches into temples of a cultural religion.

10. Frequently the need for additional space to accommodate more people is seen as an immediate price of growth. Rarely is that true. Constructing new buildings rarely is a means of growth. Architectural evangelism does not work. Building, remodeling, or adding more space should be seen as a response to growth, not as a means of achieving growth.

While this is not a complete list of the price tags on church growth, these ten items demonstrate the need for operational decisions that are consistent with the desire to grow.

The assimilation of new members and church growth can be seen as two sides of the same coin. Unfortunately, however, in too many congregations the goal of new member recruitment is perceived as an end in itself—sometimes for sound evangelistic reasons, too often for institutional maintenance and institutional goals.

The central thesis of this book is that it is un-Christian for a congregation to seek new members unless it is also willing and able to accept them into that called-out community. This is not always easy and rarely is it automatic. This closing chapter is intended to raise caution signs for those who seek church growth without looking at the costs or consequences. It is placed last to symbolize the importance of congregations, looking first at their ability to assimilate new members before embarking on an excessively simplistic church growth campaign that may produce a large proportion of inactive, alienated, and disenchanted people from among the new members and cause the long-time members to feel defeated, disillusioned, and rejected.